Flower Arrangement:

The Ikebana Way

A rikka *arrangement in an antique copper vase for* rikka *by Senei Ikenobo.*

Flower Arrangement:

The Ikebana Way

By Minobu Ohi, Senei Ikenobo,
Houn Ohara and Sofu Teshigahara

Edited by Dr. William C. Steere,
President, New York Botanical Garden

SHUFUNOTOMO CO., LTD.
Tokyo, Japan

First printing, 1972
Ninth printing, 1985

Published by Shufunotomo Co., Ltd.
2-9, Kanda Surugadai, Chiyoda-ku, Tokyo, Japan
Copyright © 1962, 1972 by Shufunotomo Co., Ltd.
Printed in Japan

ISBN4–07–970081–4

CONTENTS

PREFACE

When Buddhism was introduced into Japan about the middle of the Sixth Century, A.D., it must have been superimposed upon an earlier naturalistic religion with whose philosophy it had much in common. Otherwise, we would find it almost impossible to explain the immediate acceptance and rapid spread of the concepts, customs, and rituals of Buddhism in Japan. Thus, the practice of offering floral arrangements to Buddha by the early Chinese Buddhist priests obviously found a sympathetic reception by the Japanese people, who were apparently already using flowers in a religious context.

The symbolism and tradition of the early altar arrangements formed the basis for the art of *Ikebana*; they were later formalized into the first school of *Ikebana*, the Ikenobo School, which still flourishes. Through the centuries the concept of *Ikebana* was gradually modified and expanded from its original status as an entirely religious ceremonial activity to a broader interpretation that permitted its use for non-religious ornamental and decorative purposes, at first only by the nobility, but later by all Japanese.

In spite of the great popularization of *Ikebana* in Japan, a strong overtone of tradition and symbolism still persists, and the religious and philosophical origins of *Ikebana* have by no means been forgotten. An important feature of many oriental religions and philosophies is the sense of the oneness of man with nature; he shares the universe with plants and animals and is not in conflict with them, as, unfortunately, is too often true in Western cultures. Flower arranging to the Japanese is a special way of life, with a traditional background of spiritual and philosophical meaning; to them *Ikebana* harmonizes the laws of nature and of humanity. The traditional use of three branches, flowers, or other objects in some styles of *Ikebana* to symbolize heaven (*shin*), earth (*tai*), and man (*soe*), thus symbolizes also the whole universe.

Ikebana means literally the bringing to life of plants, and its basis is the re-creation, in a microcosm, of plants and flowers in their own natural wild settings, ranging from faithful detail to only a faint suggestion. *Ikebana* assumes on the part of the arranger and of the viewer a thorough understanding of the form and growth habits of plants during the four seasons of the year—without this understanding there cannot exist the same depth of emotional involvement. Thus, in a composition of the utmost simplicity, verging to the point of understatement, a skilled *Ikebana* arranger can suggest with a few lines not only the whole universe, but he can also create a sense of space, of motion, of time past and future, of season, of rhythm, of emotion, and of other equally diverse concepts. Lines are centrally important to *Ikebana* for the communication of its meaning, just as any object is first recognized by its lines. Much has been written on the significance of lines in *Ikebana*, as each variation in form and style has its own individual or special meaning, and these in combination can tell a whole story to one who has been properly trained to receive the message. The nature, direction, and number of lines are especially significant in suggesting a wide range of emotions and states of mind. Unlike much Western flower arranging, color is used more to complement and to reinforce line and design, but not to replace them for its own sake—although, of course, harmony in color is essential to *Ikebana*.

The gradual release through the centuries of *Ikebana* from the control exerted on it by early religious and philosophic considerations and the introduction of Western customs and plants into Japan have combined to bring about much creative experimentation and outright invention of new forms and styles. Although relatively modern, the innovative styles of the Ohara and Sogetsu Schools, both founded within the Twentieth Century, still reflect clearly their origin in the harmony and the contrast of more traditional styles. However, some of the still more recent abstract, non-realistic, or free-style designs and styles that are being taught currently by several modern Japanese schools can hardly be considered to be "flower arranging" in the usual sense, because they may lack entirely any recognizable plant materials and consist only of metal, ceramic and other man-made artifacts that lack the subtle harmonies and contrasts of traditional materials. These modern non-representational forms bear much the same relationship to classical *Ikebana* that some of the more extreme forms of modern art have to traditional art in the Western world—and we find the same elements of exaggeration, humor and "spoof."

This book, which presents the views of the headmasters of three of the most outstanding schools of *Ikebana* in Japan, will give the reader a sense of the seriousness, the creativity, the great flexibility of symbolism and ritualism, and the underlying communication of emotion inherent in *Ikebana*. One will find here comprehensive statements on the history of *Ikebana*, the philosophy of formalized *Ikebana* of the Ikenobo School, and the presentation of the concepts of two relatively modern styles, the Ohara School and the Sogetsu School, that reflect to some degree the Westernization of Japan, or perhaps more accurately, the presence now in Japan of Western flowers, and the demand by Westerners for adaptations of traditional styles of *Ikebana* for the special needs of the Western world. At first sight, it may appear that undue overlapping exists in the coverage of topics discussed by the proponents of the different schools of *Ikebana*. However, any duplication is more apparent than real, and should be considered as complementary or mutually reinforcing, since careful scrutiny will reveal that the subtle philosophical distinctions between the different schools naturally results in a somewhat different interpretation and treatment of the same forms, styles, and materials.

Anyone may enjoy the contemplation of *Ikebana*, regardless of the level of his experience or knowledge concerning this art form. However, it is perfectly obvious that the deeper are one's insights into *Ikebana*, the greater will be his understanding of the philosophical concepts and the emotional message intended by the arranger to be conveyed by his composition—and to give such insights is the purpose of this book.

William Campbell Steere

The New York Botanical Garden

8

THE
HISTORY OF
IKEBANA

By Minobu Ohi

Translated by Seiko Aoyama

Ikebana is an art conceived by the inspiration and desire of humanity to capture, interpret and enhance, with creative imagination and artistry, the beauty of the living "Way of Flowers." Historical records of *Ikebana* as an established art date from the middle of the fifteenth century (the Muromachi Period), beginning with the *rikka* or *tatebana*, meaning "standing arrangement."

Later, during the Azuchi-Momoyama Period (1560–1600), there developed the *nageire* style ("thrown-in" arrangement), and during the Edo Period (1603–1867), the *seika* style (also called *ryugibana*). Since the beginning of the Meiji Era in 1868, new styles such as *moribana* (arrangement in a low, shallow container), *jiyubana* (free arrangement) and *zen'eibana* (avant-garde arrangement) have appeared one after another. At present, *Ikebana* enjoys a most colorful variety.

Thus, with the passage of time, the art of flower arrangement has experienced gradual but significant changes. This is perhaps because *Ikebana*, being so closely connected with man's daily life, largely reflects the way of living in each different period. For example, the emergence of the *zen'eibana*, an attempt to liberate *Ikebana* from the *tokonoma* (alcove), seems to be a natural development when we consider modern architectural styles.

While such traditional art forms as *No* drama, *Chanoyu* (tea ceremony) and *Kodo* (incense burning) have rigidly retained their original characteristics, *Ikebana* has adapted itself to an advancing society by producing styles suited to the times. This, however, was not just the course of nature, but the result of our predecessors' constant creative efforts to keep pace with an ever-changing environment. The following pages trace the development of *Ikebana* through the course of time, as it is found in historical materials of various forms, to present a general idea of the background of the art of flower arrangement.

9

The Origin of *Ikebana*

In the history of floral art, its origin is said to be in *kuge* (floral offering to Buddha), a custom brought to Japan with the introduction of Buddhism in the sixth century. Some say Prince Shotoku (574–662) who helped Buddhism to establish itself as an influential religion in Japan, originated the art of flower arrangement. This of course supports the belief that its source is found in the custom of *kuge*.

The idea of offering flowers to Buddha was readily accepted and cherished by the Japanese people, as the ground had been favorably cultivated. In *Nihon Shoki*, the oldest chronicles of Japan, we find "Every plant can well express itself." This reveals not only the primitive people's animism, but also the fact that they felt some mysterious life latent in plants. This mysterious aura was even more deeply felt in the unchanging evergreens than in short-lived seasonal plants. Accordingly, the *sakaki*, an evergreen, was offered to gods on all ceremonial occasions. This custom still persists in the Shinto rites.

Again in the *Nihon Shoki* we find the episode recorded that when the goddess Izanami died and was entombed, the natives of the place offered flowers of the season to console her soul. We should recognize this as historical proof of the existence of the custom of offering flowers prior to the introduction of Buddhism into Japan.

Japan's mild climate with its four changing seasons encourages a natural terrain rich in a great variety of blooming flowers. It was quite natural, therefore, for our predecessors to cultivate an appreciation of the beauty of flowers. It was this native affection for flowers which moved the ancient Japanese to willingly accept the Buddhist flower-offering custom. In turn, their own interest in flowers was greatly encouraged. We can say, therefore, that the history of *Ikebana* began with the custom of *kuge* and developed along with it.

Rikka arrangement from "Senkaden-hisho."

Daibutsu *at the Todai-ji Temple.*

FLOWERS OFFERED TO BUDDHA

An example of the renchi.
(The Shoso-in Treasure Depository)

As Buddhism prospered in the late seventh century, the custom of *kuge* became prevalent at temples. It appears that the people felt Buddha's all-saving power in the grand beauty of the floral offerings used as *shogon* (ornaments before a Buddhist altar).

In 752, when the Emperor Shomu performed the dedication ceremony of Todai-ji Temple, the priests offered flowers to *Daibutsu* (Great Buddha) who was enshrined there. On this occasion, lotus, the official Buddhist flower, was used. People arranged these flowers in a *keko* (basket) or a *keban* (basin). Some artificial lotus flowers called *renchi* were also used.

11

An example of kuge *in which lotus flowers are offered on lotus leaves, from the picture "Shojuraigo." (The Kongobu-ji Temple at Mt. Koya)*

In the tenth century, as the Jodo sect of Buddhism became prevalent, *kuge* began to play a decorative role, for in this sect the ideal place was the *Gokuraku-Jodo* (the land of perfect bliss) which was imagined to be full of flowers. If we look at the ancient picture "*Shojuraigo*" (paradise) of the eleventh century, we see the grand gorgeousness of *kuge* well represented. In the offering scene some heavenly maidens hold in both hands lotus flowers arranged in a *keban*. Another picture shows a standing figure holding a vase of lotus flowers. In *Itsukushima-Heike-Nokyo*, an illustrated sutra of the late twelfth century, some peony-like flowers with leaves are depicted arranged in a vase. From these examples it is clear that *kuge* showed various trends.

Section of the Honen-Shonin-Picture-Scroll.

The Eleven-faced Kannon.
(*The Domyo-ji Temple in Kawachi*)

A gilt bronze vase.
(*The Kanshin-ji Temple*)

Detail of a stone bas-relief. (*The Fusai-ji Temple*)

Coming to the Kamakura Period (1192–1333) we find lotus flowers offered in vases, as seen in the *Honen-Shonin-Picture-Scroll*, and in the gilded bronze flower vases of the Kanshin-ji Temple. Other relics such as *itabi* (a kind of tombstone) also show floral offerings as done in those days. In the *itabi* of the Fusai-ji Temple, dated the first year of Koan (1278), lotus flowers are depicted in a vase. Here the main lotus stem stands at the center, with similar flowers arranged symmetrically on either side, resembling a pattern of design. This *itabi* was in the form of *kuge* which was most popular among the ordinary people of the time.

On the other hand, among the aristocratic people, celadon vases imported through the Japan-Sung trade were highly esteemed. These vases were of various sizes, some of them being so large that only big plants could be arranged in them. In such vases, a few large and attractive cherry branches were often used, or a few delicate flowers gracefully arranged around a single large pine branch. These arrangements were for the appreciation of privileged aristocrats. It is presumed that the structure of these arrangements owed much to the influence of contemporary painting (e.g. *Kasuga-Gongen-Kenki*).

This influence continued through the next Muromachi Period (1336–1573).

A celadon vase. (The Kanazawa Library)

A scene in the Kasuga-Gongen-Kenki-Picture-Scroll, *which suggests to us that the structure of nature had influence upon the* rikka *style.*

Pine and Camellia trees. A garden scene in the Boki-E-Kotoba-Scrolls.

A good example is seen in the garden scene painted in the *Boki-E-Kotoba-Scrolls*, partially painted in 1351 and added to in 1482. Also shown in the scrolls is the structure of a *"bonsan"* (miniature garden) which reveals its relation to the *rikka* style.

Under such circumstances, the flower arrangement which was primarily of religious origin, keeping the form of *mitsugusoku* before the Buddhist altar, gradually changed its nature, and flowers came to be arranged for the appreciation of people. When this tendency became a custom, arranging flowers began to develop as an art.

The *mitsugusoku* is a set for floral offering, consisting of an incense burner flanked by a candlestick on one side and a vase of flowers on the other, the whole thing being placed on the *oshi-ita* (an earlier style of alcove). A picture from the *Boki-E-Kotoba-Scrolls* shows a room in which three pictures hang on the front wall with an incense burner placed before them. On either side of the incense burner is a vase containing pine branches. This formation deviates from the exact Buddhist form by omitting the candlestick and adopting a new design in general.

An example of a bonsan *from the* Boki-E-Kotoba-Scrolls.

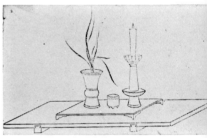

An example of an oshi-ita *from a page of the* Kokka, *No. 28.*

Pine branch arrangement in front of the hanging scrolls depicting the plum and the bamboo; a picture in the Boki-E-Kotoba-Scrolls.

A vase containing cherry branches which is placed in front of a wooden sliding door;
a scene from the Boki-E-Kotoba-Scrolls.

Another picture in the same scrolls shows an example of a modified form of the *mitsugusoku*, with cherry branches arranged in a vase placed before a wooden sliding door. From one branch hangs a strip of paper bearing a *waka* poem, for the benefit of poetry lovers. Still another vase containing flowers and placed in an alcove appears in the same scrolls.

A tokonoma *in which is displayed a vase of flowers. Section of the* Boki-E-Kotoba-Scrolls.

THE ESTABLISHMENT OF FLORAL ART

A scene of the kusa-awase *depicted on a fan-paper.*

A bronze container.

It was at the *tanabata-hana-awase* (a floral competition held at Star Festival) that flowers first became the theme of an annual event. The *tanabata-hana-awase* dates from the time of Yoshimitsu Ashikaga (1358–1408), the third Ashikaga *shogun* and famous as the founder of the Kinkaku-ji Temple (Golden Pavilion). He loved flowers so much and had so many celebrated flowers planted in his garden that people referred to his mansion as "the palace of flowers."

The *hana-awase* (a floral competition) followed tradition from the Heian Period. It was of the same character as the *nadeshiko-awase* (a competition of wild pinks), the *shobu-ne-awase* (a competition of the length of iris roots), and the *kusa-awase* (a competition of various grasses). The *tanabata-hana-awase* had the significance of *kuge,* offering flowers to the two stars, *kengyu* (Altair) and *shokujo* (Vega). On this occasion, nearly one hundred vases of *sennoge* decorated with their beautiful colors. Here the *shogun,* the room and the whole atmosphere was aglow

A samurai's *room described in the picture* "Shuhanron.

noblemen, priests and *samurai* banqueted and enjoyed themselves. Later the flowers arranged for the *tanabata-hana-awase* were displayed to be viewed by the general public. Thus, the flowers seen at the *tanabata-hana-awase* tended to become a public pleasure rather than a dedication to the stars.

Further studies of flower arranging resulted, in the middle of the fifteenth century, in the crystallization of the *rikka* or *tatebana* style as the first step in its establishment as an art. The *rikka* arrangement of those days was usually composed around a pine branch as the *shin*—the main branch standing in the center—regardless of the season. Occasionally a plum branch or Japanese cypress limb was used for the *shin*. The relative positions of the various stems used in a typical

rikka arrangement were fixed as follows:

Around the *shin*, groups of stems were placed respectively to the right, to the left, to the front, to the lower right, to the left rear, to the right front, to the lower front, and at the base. Nomenclature such as *soe* or *soe-uke* for identification of the principal branches did not exist at that time.

The *rikka* arrangement was done in one of the three styles known as *shin*, *gyo* and *so*. In the *shin* style, the *shin* branch and the groups of other branches were arranged in a bronze container. The *gyo* style was typically a low arrangement of considerable breadth, done in a wide, shallow container filled with sand. In the *so* style, which was also called *nageire*, flowers were arranged in a boat-shaped hanging container.

Rikka

THE ARRANGERS OF *RIKKA*

What kind of people arranged flowers in the *rikka* style in its early period? The *rikka* arrangers were chiefly such men as *doboshu* (priests) and *zassho* (court noblemen's retainers).

Doboshu who did diverse services for the *shogun* were especially good at art and won from him a generous patronage. Primarily priests of the Jishu sect of Buddhism, they held the title of *ami*. Among them, Ryuami, Soami and Mon'ami were the most eminent masters of the *rikka* style.

Ryuami was a retainer of Yoshimasa Ashikaga (1435–1490), the eighth Ashikaga *shogun*. He would often execute a magnificent *rikka* arrangement to the *shogun*'s liking and stood high in his favor.

Soami had a deep knowledge of *zashiki-kazari* (interior decoration) and was excellent in the *rikka* arrangements, too.

Mon'ami wrote a text on the *rikka* style. It is said that his arranging was so expert that flowers arranged by him appeared as if growing from the ground. He could arrange flowers tastefully for any occasion, festive or condolatory, and won the highest praise from the *shogun* and the court noblemen.

In these ways the *doboshu* endeavored to master the *rikka* style to *shoguns'* approval and contributed in no small measure to the development of floral art. Their style of arrangement became so popular that it stands alone as representative of those times.

By the middle of the sixteenth century, however, they had given place to the Ikenobo masters. This was historically inevitable when we recall that they were patronized by *shoguns*. At the time of Yoshimasa Ashikaga—the central figure of the Higashiyama culture and a great patron of the *rikka* style—there occurred in Kyoto the Civil War of Onin, which was to last eleven years. The cause of this war was Yoshimasa's indifference to affairs of state and consequent loss of political power. A natural result of his ruin was the shift of the center of floral art from *doboshu* to the Ikenobo masters.

On the other hand, priests were undoubtedly men of high culture in their day and the custom of *kuge* afforded them ample opportunity to handle and appreciate flowers. Of the many eminent flower arrangers to come from among this class after the beginning of the fifteenth century, Ikenobo Senkei of the Rokkaku-do Temple in Kyoto was the best known.

In 1462, at the request of a *samurai*, Senkei did a *rikka* style arrangement in a gold vase, his wonderful skill causing a sensation among the people of Kyoto. Ikenobo Senjun, who was a linked-verse poet, also ranked among the first Ikenobo masters.

The Rokkaku-do Temple which produced these great masters was one of the Buddhist amulet-issuing offices. Easily accessible to people, it was visited by pilgrims from all over the country. It was here that the *rikka* style of the Ikenobo school, which was more appealing to the general tastes, was born and replaced that developed by the *doboshu*.

Thus by the beginning of the seventeenth century the Ikenobo school had been firmly established and enjoyed a virtual monopoly in the domain of floral art.

Another eminent flower master of the time was the *samurai* Hisamori Osawa, who was one of the retainers of the court nobleman Tokikuni Yamashina. He flourished in the art from 1488 to 1492. At court with his master, he arranged flowers in the *rikka* style for alcoves and cabinets of such rooms as *ko-gosho* (a council room), *kuroto-gosho* (a room for poetry parties) and *gogakumon-jo* (a study). His arrangements were highly esteemed as decorations among the people of the court. One of his arrangements was as follows: Using a branch of hatchet-leaved arborvitae as the *shin*, a branch of cypress and some *hiyakushun* were arranged at the front. Some grass covered the base as *shitakusa* (undergrowth). In another of his arrangements, a plum branch was used as the *shin*, with a cypress branch as a supporting branch at the left front. Narcissi and leaves were grouped at the front, with a coltsfoot and marigolds to their left. Still another example shows a

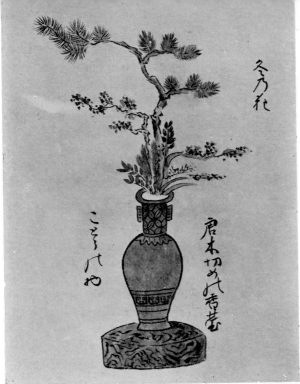

冬乃花

こそ尺れ

唐木切め此香堂

The Mon'ami-no-Densho, *written in the middle 16th century.*

A scene from the play "Hajitomi."

pine branch used as the *shin*. A root of the same tree, from which stretched a long branch, was placed to the left of the *shin*, some red plum blossoms to the right. At the base, a coltsfoot and marigolds, *akamirotis* and some grasses as the *shitakusa* were arranged. These are representative of the *rikka* style arrangements of those days.

The increasing number of skilled flower arrangers of the *rikka* style gave further impetus to the propagation of the art. The theme of the *kyogen* (a comic interlude) titled "Shin'ubai" concerns a *daimyo* (feudal lord) who goes to Higashiyama in Kyoto to look for a branch suitable for the *shin* of a *rikka* arrangement. The *No* play "Hajitomi" contains the scene of a *rikka-kuyo* (a mass for the dead marked by many *rikka* arrangements). These examples reveal the acceptance and familiarity of *rikka* style flower arrangements in the daily life of the common people. Among *samurai* families, this popularity led to the use of vases to decorate the alcove, and occasionally as gifts or even as pawns.

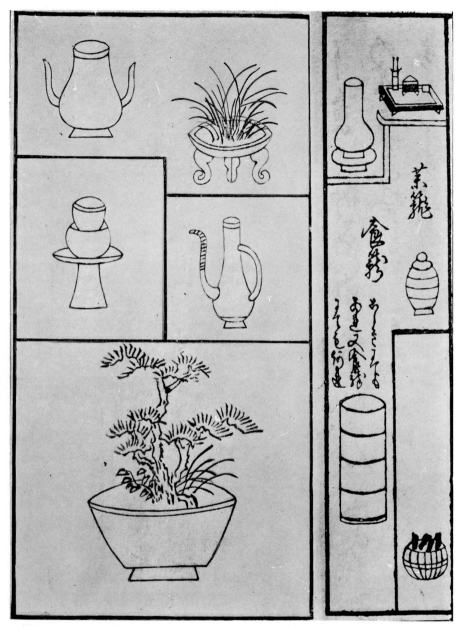

Detail of the Sendensho.

As the floral art developed and prevailed, texts were written in response to demands for more information. The oldest such work, known as *Sendensho*, is the compilation of texts covering the years from 1445 to 1536. It is itemized; however it lacks unity. Contained in it are instructions for fifty-three arrangements for various occasions such as *genpuku-no-hana* (celebration of a boy's coming of age), *shutsujin-no-hana* (the *samurai*'s

departure for the front), *muko-yome-tori-no-hana* (wedding), and *mitsugusoku-no-hana* (offering to Buddha). For example, on the *samurai*'s departure for the front, flowers such as camellias which fall easily should not be used, being suggestive of death in battle. Flowers of four colors or of four kinds were forbidden because the Japanese word "*shi*" (four) has the same phonetic sound as "*shi*" (death). From such examples we

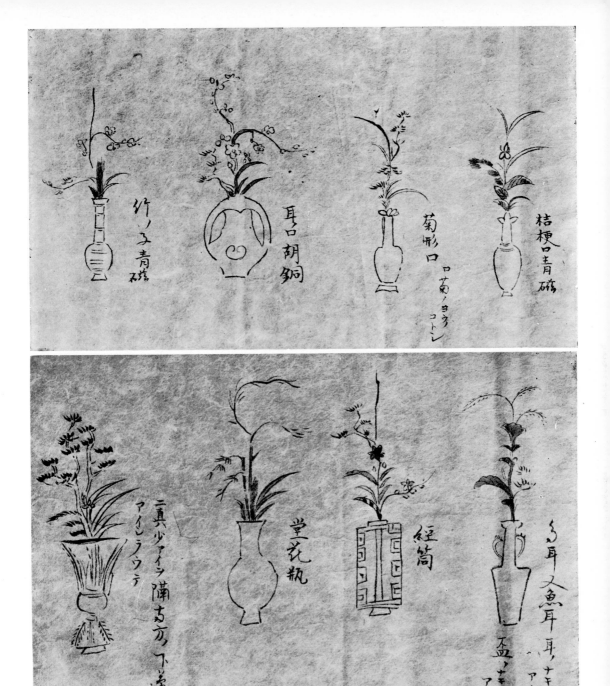

Examples of rikka *arrangement in 1554. (The Yomei Library)*

understand that flower arrangement was a recognized means of expression of human feelings. *Rikka* style arrangement was regarded also as a symbolic representation of nature.

The *Sendensho*, in its conclusion, stresses the importance of practice to improve skill in the art, stating that the arranger might attain a good command of flowers only through diligent practice. *Keiko* (practice) is regarded as essential also in such traditional art forms of medieval origin as *No* drama, *Chanoyu and Kodo.*

The *Mon'ami-no-Densho*, written by Mon'ami, more systematic and more advanced in theory than the *Sendensho*, contains a preface and a Buddhist interpretation of the art. Texts on floral art, however, reveal a gradual inclination towards secrecy.

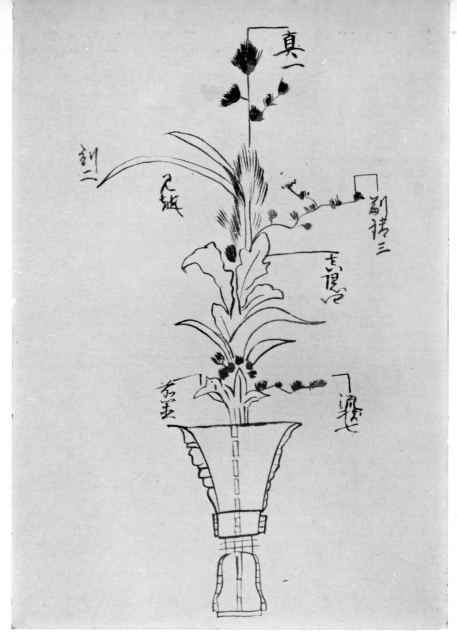

The Ikenobo-Sen'ei-Densho, *dated 1545.*

The *Senno-kuden*, written in 1542, reorganized the foregoing two books. The author, Senno, an Ikenobo master, arranged flowers at Court in 1532 and became famous for his wonderful skill. He teaches in his book the technique of presenting picturesque scenery in a short time by means of some water in a receptacle and small cuttings of plants, and strongly advocates the Ikenobo school. Other succeeding texts were also written by Ikenobo masters indicating that the Ikenobo school maintained the authoritative position achieved by Master Senkei.

In 1545, the *Ikenobo-Sen'ei-Densho* was written.

It formulated for the first time the regular principles of the *rikka* style, giving the nomenclature of the seven principal branches as follows: *shin* ("true, straight" branch standing in the center), *soe* ("supporting" branch), *soe-uke* ("receiving" branch), *shin-kakushi* ("hiding" branch), *mae-oki* ("anterior" branch) and *nagashi-eda* ("flowing" branch).

Another text appeared in 1554, in which the *rikka* arrangement appears in a *kikyoguchi* (vase with a mouth shaped like a Chinese bellflower) of celadon make, as well as in a bronze container with handles.

The grand hall in the Nishi-Hongan-ji Temple.

RIKKA AND *NAGEIRE* IN THE MOMOYAMA PERIOD

After the Civil War of Onin, many court noble-men left the war-devastated city of Kyoto to seek a living in the country. In this way many aspects of urban culture spread into the country, and *rikka* was no exception. Feudal lords and their retainers, regarding it of equal importance to their martial skill, attempted mastery of the art. Texts continued to be written one after another, helping to promote the spread of the art through the countryside.

The brilliant Momoyama Period (1560–1600) followed the long confusion resulting from the war. This era was characterized, among other things, by the construction of magnificent castles. The *rikka*-style arrangement was considered a most appropriate interior decoration for such castles, and became even more majestic in order to suit the purpose. No less decorative than the brilliant pictures found on walls and doors of the great halls, *rikka* enjoyed a flourishing popularity.

A picture of cherry blossoms.
(The Chijaku-in Temple)

A new style of flower arrangement appeared during this period, to form a striking contrast to the *rikka* style. In the middle of the sixteenth century, *Sen-no-Rikyu* (1520–1591), the founder of the tea ceremony, succeeded in developing an original style of flower arrangement as a necessary adjunct to the tea ceremony. Known as *nageire* (thrown-in style), it is also called *chabana* (tea arrangement), because of its close association with *Chanoyu* (tea ceremony). He wrote in his book that only one or two kinds of flowers should be arranged as naturally "as if they were growing in a field."

According to him, tea ceremony is "only a matter of making a fire, boiling water and drinking tea." The words stress spiritual joy experienced through "simpleness." This simplicity is also characteristic of the *chabana*. The container was called *hanaire* meaning "to put in flowers" and various devices were created to emphasize simpleness with originality. The container known as *take-no-hanaire* was made by Sen-no-Rikyu from bamboo of Nirayama on the Izu Peninsula during his service in Hideyoshi's attack on Odawara.

As for the flowers themselves, simple, light-hued ones were considered to be appropriate. Flowers of only one variety were generally used in an arrangement: iris blooms thrown in the bamboo container, single-petaled white peach blossoms arranged in a basket container, or a single chrysanthemum in a slender vase. In arranging, the

From a book on rikka-*style*
arrangement, dated 1582.
(Author's collection)

arranger's state of mind was considered most important.

To illustrate this point there is recorded a famous episode concerning Rikyu. One day, Hideyoshi Toyotomi (1536–1598), the master of the entire land in those days, heard about the beautiful morning glories in full bloom in Rikyu's garden. When he came to see them, he was disappointed to see none in the garden, but when he entered the tea ceremony room a single morning glory, beautifully composed, filled him with great admiration, and he recognized the single flower as a symbol of the beauty of the flower-filled garden. Thus insight and discernment were required of an arranger of flowers.

Hitoe-gire *or* take-no-hanaire, *one-level bamboo container made by Sen-no-Rikyu.*

Chabana *arrangements and vases depicted by Sotan Kamiya in his diary.*

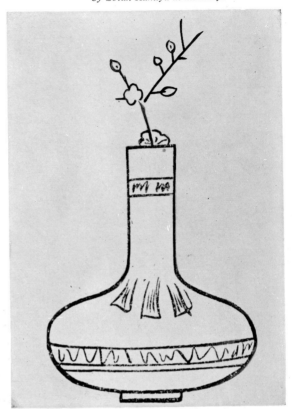

Kinuta-seiji-hoo-mimi-hanaike, *celadon vase with handles which embody a phoenix.*

There were no special rules regarding the *chabana,* simpleness being the essential principle applied to both flowers and vases. Vases known as *kinuta-seiji* (celadon vases in the shape of a tamping tool) were highly valued for their neatness and simplicity.

Sotan Kamiya (1551–1635), one of Rikyu's pupils, records *chabana* arrangements in his diary. They are marvelously simple arrangements. In the tea ceremony room light-colored flowers were preferred as being in better harmony with the various tea utensils.

Rikka arrangements for the tea ceremony, especially when held in the *shoin-zukuri* room (a room following the architectural style of a study), usually consisted of only one kind of flowers. These were called *isshiki-rikka* ("one-color" arrangements). Later, however, *isshiki-rikka* style was extended to general *rikka* arrangement, showing the influence of the *chabana.* In the Edo Period, the simple *nageire* style of the *chabana* became popular. From it was to develop the *seika* style.

Artificial camellia flowers used for decoration of the furyugasa *in the picture "Hokoku-sai Festival," 1604*

FESTIVALS AND FLOWERS

During festival celebrations at shrines and when *Bon*-festival dances were in progress, it was the custom to parade the streets carrying a *furyugasa*, a parasol decorated with paper-made ornaments to attract the public gaze.

On the seventh memorial day of Hideyoshi Toyotomi observed in 1604, a special *Hokoku-sai* festival was held. On this occasion poeple made imitations of such floral combinations as a pine branch entwined with wisteria flowers, camellias arranged in a receptacle, and a standing cherry branch. These were used to decorate the *furyu-gasa*, and much attention was attracted to the designs, which were suggestive of the *rikka* style. From this time, festivals and *furyugasa* were always found together, and flower sellers in Kyoto became popular and prosperous.

The furyugasa *at the memorial service held at Imamiya in Murasakino, Kyoto. Section of the illustrated* Miyako-Meisho.

POPULARITY OF *RIKKA*

At the beginning of the seventeenth century—the early part of the Edo Period—the *rikka* style of flower arrangement developed conspicuously through the efforts of the Ikenobo master Senko and many other skilled flower arrangers. Senko's pupils included priests and merchants, and Ishin Daijuin of the Honno-ji Temple ranked first among them, being mentioned with high praise for the splendor of his arrangements.

A rikka *arrangement done by Ishin Daijuin in 1678.*

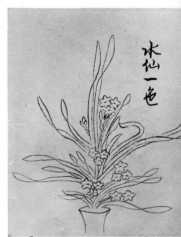

An example of the suisen-
isshiki, *a* rikka *arrangement
composed solely of narcissus.*

From "Rikka Arrangements
of the Rokkakudo Ikeno-
bo and Its Disciples" *dated
1673, an example of the
hundred arrangements found
in the book.*

It was at this time that the tendency towards the *isshiki-rikka*, a direct influence of the *chabana,* was first exhibited in the *rikka* style. As stated earlier, *isshiki-rikka* arrangements were composed of a single variety of material. Pine branches, cherry blossoms, or narcissi might be used; however each was arranged separately and alone.

In the latter part of the seventeenth century the *rikka* style became better regulated. "*Rikka Arrangements of the Rokkakudo Ikenobo and Its Disciples*" was published in 1673, and contained

illustrations of Senko's and his pupils' representative arrangements as models of the *rikka* style.

In 1683 the *Rikka Taizen* (Encyclopedia of *Rikka*) was published by Tauemon Juichiya, one of Senko's students. This was a complete and systematic study of the *rikka* style, giving the nomenclature of the main branches as *shin, soe, uke* ("receiving" branch), *nagashi-eda, mae-oki, do-zukuri* ("body" or "trunk"), *hikae-eda* ("waiting" branch). As the *rikka* style came to be regulated in this manner, its pattern naturally became too set, formal and rigid to permit expression of original ideas by arrangers.

The *Rikka Jiseisho* (Styles of Current *Rikka*), dated 1688, says "The *shin* dominates like a sovereign and the six other branches attend it like subjects." Indeed the orderly form of the *rikka* style suggests the feudalistic relationship of master and servants. In this fact lay the source of the educational role of floral art in those days, and the art of flower arrangement, like calligraphy, came to be regarded as one of women's necessary accomplishments.

Part of the Rikka Taizen.

An early 18th century scene depicting an arranger of rikka *at work*.

A scene showing women occupied with calligraphy. Note an arrangement of a single chrysanthemum, drawn by Harunobu Suzuki.

The rikka *arrangements displayed at* tanabata *in the Nishi-Hongan-ji Temple.*

It was at this time that the word "*kado*," meaning floral art with a bit of moralistic shade, was used for the first time. This sustains the belief that *rikka* had become systematized and had attained a definite role in society.

As floral art continued to develop, it spread not only among priests, nobles and *samurai*, but also among the people of the lower class. Many people took lessons in flower arrangement.

Rikka retained its popularity through the beginning of the seventeenth century. With the establishment of the feudal system, the *chonin* (merchant) class began to gain in economic power. Becoming also the support and driving force of culture, it was soon to replace the court noblemen and *samurai*.

In 1629, at the command of the ex-Emperor Go-mizu-no-O, an exhibition of *rikka* arrangements was held at the Court. It was an unusual exhibition in that it was open to priests and merchants as well as to court noblemen. This served to further increase of the popularity of floral art among the rich merchant class.

According to the *Rikka-Shodo-shu* (1684), many people both high and low attempted mastery of the art, and the latter part of the seventeenth century became the Golden Age of the *rikka* style.

At Star Festival people went to the Hongan-ji Temple to see the *rikka* and the *kagobana* (flowers arranged in a basket) exhibited for the occasion.

KABUKI AND *RIKKA*

In 1717, the *Shotoku-Taishi-Edenki* (Pictorial Biography of Prince Shotoku) by Monzaemon Chikamatsu was presented at the Takemoto-za theater in Osaka. In the play, actors spoke the lines used by people in describing *rikka* arrangements. For example: "Oh, beautiful! Reeds are used as the *shin*. The *soe* is a branch of willow. Winter chrysanthemums form the *mae-oki* and a cockscomb flower the *sho-shin*, with some graceful branches supporting it." Such technical words as "*rokka-rokuyo, shika-shiyo*" (six flowers and six leaves, four flowers and four leaves) were heard in the play. The audiences of those days could understand such terms well enough to enjoy the play. Even in the gay quarters, the *rikka* style of flower arrangement was very popular.

As previously mentioned, the writers of the texts of the *rikka* style were of the *chonin* class. The *rikka* arrangements done by Senkei Fushunken, the author of *Rikka Jiseisho*, were especially noteworthy, as they reflected the tastes of the merchant class in the late seventeenth century. He opposed the traditional, complicated rules governing the *rikka* structure, used branches of unusual shape, and displayed a versatile skill in his arrangements. Finally he broke away from the Ikenobo school. His curious and varied compositions appealed to the public tastes and he enjoyed great popularity among rich merchants. The *rikka* style, however, remained unchanged, discouraging any originality on the part of its arrangers.

Flower Arrangement in the Genroku Period

During the Genroku Period (1688–1703) the merchant class made great advances in the economic field and found its way into the cultural sphere of the community.

In the field of floral art, the *nageire* style began to replace rigidly formal *rikka*. By the close of the seventeenth century the great popularity which had heretofore been enjoyed by the *rikka* style began to diminish because or its inflexible and complicated rules and difficulty in obtaining suitable materials. There then appeared the new style *nageirebana* to meet the demand for a simpler form of flower arrangement.

The *nageire* as *chabana* had spread widely with tea ceremony since the late sixteenth century. At this stage of its development, however, it became independent of tea ceremony and made its debut as one of the *Ikebana* styles.

From the Seiro-Bijin-Aisugata-Kagami, *a* geisha *doing a* nageire *arrangement and a* tokonoma *with* nageire *arrangements on the dais and the post.*

35

A page of the Seiro-Bijin-Aisugata-Kagami *which shows* geisha*s viewing a* rikka *arrangement.*

The picture "Furuy-Soka-kai," *showing an exhibition of* seika *arrangements, painted by Choki Eishosai in the late 18th century.*

The *nageire* had no special rules in its early days. It was so free and easy a style that it appealed to the public fancy. Sometimes *nageire* arrangements were used to decorate the alcoves of even the common people. Gradually, a demand arose for *nageire* arrangements of refined appearance to suit the alcove.

According to the *Nageire Kishi-no-Nami* dated 1740, *nageirebana* at this time included any type of arrangement other than those done in the *rikka* style. The book gives three styles of *nageirebana;* the *seika* (three branch asymmetrical style), the *nageire* (single flower *chabana* style) and the *ike komi* (many flowers thrown in as naturally as possible). The *seika* is mentioned as a suitable style for a *shoin-zukuri* room (study) or a large room, the *nageire* for a tea ceremony room or a small room. It is apparent that in the early eighteenth century the *seika* was regarded as an appropriate style for the alcove, being included in the *nageirebana*. An *Ukiyo-e* print of those days depicts an *ikekomi* arrangement of many chrysanthemums done in a basket container.

In the late eighteenth century, however, the *seika* style was placed in a different category. Combining the dignity of *rikka* with the simplicity of *nageire*, the *seika* style came into the limelight as a decoration for the alcove.

An example of a splendid container.

Chrysanthemums arranged in a basket; a picture by Shunsho Katsukawa (1726–92).

Meanwhile, different new schools of the *seika* style sprang up one after another. First there appeared such schools as the Ko-ryu, the Enshu-ryu, the Genji-ryu, the Higashiyama-ryu, and later on the Soami-ryu, the Yoken-ryu, the Furuta-ryu and the Yashiro-ryu schools followed them, and the *Ie-moto* (headmaster) system became firmly established.

These schools were active cheifly in Edo. In the latter part of the eighteenth century, the center of floral art shifted from Kyoto and Osaka to Edo. Edo had already become the center of economic activity of the merchant class. In those days, daily exhibitions of *seika* arrangements were held in Edo restaurants or other public places. Rich merchants often vied with each other in displaying splendid containers, placing less emphasis on the contained. The *seika* style arrangement was even adapted into a fabric design. It may be said that the merchants who had become richer since the Genroku Period sought an outlet for their surplus riches in *Ikebana* as well as in debauchery and play-going.

As *Ikebana* came to be regarded generally as one of the genteel accomplishments, there arose a demand for a simplified form that might be more easily taught and mastered. Thus, in the early nineteenth century, there came into existence the basic "triangle" form. This asymmetric form built up from three principal branches—symbolizing *ten* (heaven), *jin* (man), and *chi* (earth) respectively—enabled anyone to do a *seika* arrangement with ease. By this time other schools, such as the

Kimono of Kaga Yuzen *printed silk, with a pattern of* seika *style arrangements.* (*The Matsuzakaya Dyeing and Weaving Data Institute*)

An example of a "heaven-earth-man" style arrangement.

Misho-ryu and the Sekishu-ryu had come into existence. Each school introduced its own version of the *seika*, which was also referred to as *ryugi bana*.

As we have seen, the *nageirebana* style of the late seventeenth century developed into the "heaven-earth-man" *seika* style in a little over a hundred years. This was, in short, the popularization of flower arrangement reflecting the taste of the merchants who had risen to power.

Formalization of the *seika* style was a natural result of its popularity, but it was the ease and simplicity of this basic form that made *seika* ideally suited for room decoration. Marked by its popularity among women, it was regarded as one of their gracious accomplishments. By 1868, the time of the Imperial Restoration, the *seika* style dominated the field of flower arrangement, and the word "*seika*" had become a synonym for *Ikebana*.

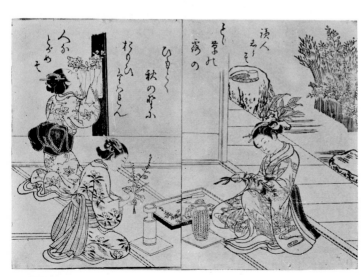

A picture from the illustrated Nippon-Fuzoku, *showing some women taking lessons in* Ikebana, *in the Edo Period.*

In the early nineteenth century, a freestyle arrangement known as *bunjin-ike*("literati" style arrangement) became popular among some of the leading artists of the day, of whom Chikuden Tanomura (1777–1835) was representative. This style was quite bold and lively, being an expression inspired by the arranger's freedom from worldly cares. This style continued to be favored by intellectuals into the early days of the Meiji Era.

Another example of a lesson in Ikebana; *a picture from the* Nippon-Jorei-shiki *in the Meiji Era.*

Flower Arrangement in the Meiji Era

A picture which shows an Ikebana *mistress, painted in the middle of the 19th century.*

With the establishment of the Meiji government in 1868, "civilization and enlightenment" began to flood various fields. The trend of this age was to discard old customs and to seek novelties.

In *Ikebana*, schools persisting in the old traditions became targets for criticism, for remaining aloof to the general trend of the age and indifferent to the imported *Yobana* (Western style of flower arrangement). Moreover, most schools were suffering an economic crisis.

In the middle of the Meiji Era, around 1887, as nationalism replaced Westernism as the prevailing influence, *Ikebana* as well as the tea ceremony enjoyed a revival as an aesthetic attainment unique to the Japanese.

In many girls' schools, flower arrangement was encouraged as part of the school curriculum for future "good wives and wise mothers." Later in the era flower arrangement was to become listed as one of women's indispensable accomplishments, and a desirable prerequisite to marriage. In the early twentieth century, flower arrangement was so popular among women that it became a female profession. Nevertheless, the new trend to break away from the traditional "heaven-earth-man" style had not yet taken firm hold.

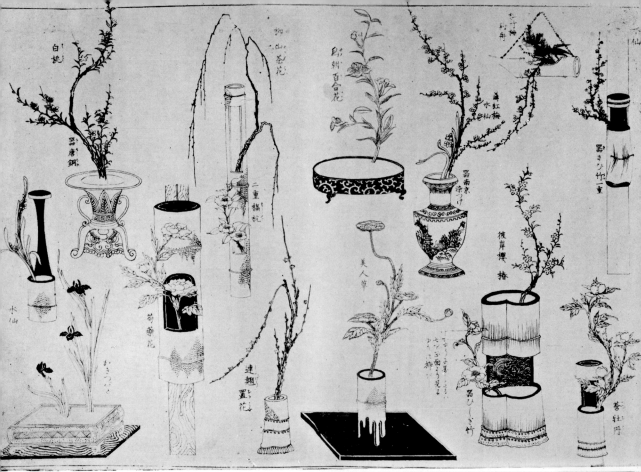

Examples of Seika *printed in "Fuzoku-Gaho"*
(1887).

Flower Arrangement of Today

While the traditional *seika* style persisted, a new and completely dissimilar style was gradually but steadily competing for popularity. Known as the *moribana* style, it was the first attempt to utilize Western flowers in Japanese arrangements. Unshin Ohara, creator of the style, founded the Ohara-ryu in 1897 and began to foster development of the theme of *moribana*, arrangements in low, shallow containers. Having color and decorative beauty, the style gained rapidly in popularity as a home arrangement.

Moribana *by Unshin Ohara (1913).*

During the Taisho Era (1912–1925) it achieved recognition equal to that of the *seika* style. Koshu Tsujii, who was one of Unshin Ohara's disciples, established the Saga-ryu at the Daikaku-ji Temple in Kyoto. Also in the early part of the Taisho Era (early twentieth century), Choka Adachi initiated an "Adachi Style," using the *moribana* form to "arrange flowers like flowers."

At about this same time, still another style, known as *bunjin-ike* ("literati") style, began to attract public interest. Originated by Issotei Nishikawa, this was a free-style, more colorful and varied than the *nageire* style. Its popularity among the intellectuals was stimulated by an organ called "*Heishi*" issued by Nishikawa. The trend towards free creative arranging, encouraged by the *moribana* and the *bunjin-ike* styles, at last brought forth the *jiyubana* (free arrangement). Representative schools of the *jiyubana* style are Bumpo Nakayama's Misho-ryu and Nakayama-Bumpo-kai.

Early in the Showa Era (the present era, which began in 1926), the influence of avant-garde art provided the vital spark needed to bring about the break with tradition that proved to be *Ikebana's* emancipation from the *tokonoma* (alcove). Modern modes of living demanded a more versatile form. Originality and creative individuality became the keynotes characterizing the style, and *Ikebana* became a formative art, utilizing not only floral materials, but various substances treated as shape, color and line. Thus *zen'eibana* came into being, to fulfill the need for an avant-garde floral art.

Bunjin-ike *by Issotei Nishikawa.*

Jiyubana *by Bumpo Nakayama (1939).*

Representative of *zen'eibana*, Sogetsu School was founded by Sofu Teshigahara in the first year of Showa (1926). Following the Pacific War (1941–1945), *zen'eibana* began to spread with astonishing rapidity, and today is an established form of *Ikebana*, in which arrangers strive always for the perfect combination of nature and art that will further enhance the natural beauty of flowers.

Briefly, the foregoing chapter outlines the historical progress of *Ikebana*. In addition to those schools mentioned earlier, some of the existing schools of *Ikebana* today are: Koryu-shoto-kai; Headmaster: *Riei Ikeda*. Misho-ryu; *Koho Hihara*. Seifu-Heika; *Shodo Hayakawa*. Kuwabara-Senkei-ryu; *Senkei Kuwabara*. Ryuseiha; *Kasen Yoshimura*. Ichiyo-shiki; *Meiko Kasuya*. Enshu-ryu; *Isshin Mori*. Shofu-ryu; *Josui Oshikawa*. Nisshin-ryu; *Nisshin Arai*. Yamato-Kado; *Ten'ei Shimoda*. Man'yo-ryu; *Manyoan Kawamura*. Senkei-ryu; *Senkei Nishizaka*. Enzan-ryu; *Gyokudo Yoshida*. Kofu-ryu; *Saigetsu Yamamoto*.

Zeneibana *by Sofu Teshigahara* (*1960*).

THE IKENOBO SCHOOL

By Senei Ikenobo

Translated by Yoshimasa Ichikawa

As the first school of *Ikebana* to be defined and formalized, The Ikenobo School was founded about the middle of the Fifteenth Century. It had its early basis in the original ceremonial art form of floral offerings for the altar introduced by Chinese Buddhist priests in the Sixth Century, in a highly rigorous intellectual and religious climate, but since then much less formal and ritualistic presentations or arrangements of flowers have evolved and have been widely accepted. The traditional styles and symbolism of the past are today enriched by novel and even daring expressions of the harmony, and, at the same time, of the contrasts of *Ikebana*. It has been said that Ikenobo is nothing but the history of *Ikebana* itself, but this statement is generally correct only if restricted to the more traditional and conservative styles of *Ikebana*— and in this restricted sense the terms are more or less interchangeable, as this chapter shows. As will be seen from Headmaster Senei Ikenobo's remarks, the Ikenobo School of today is still steeped in tradition, symbolism and philosophy.

The fundamental concepts of Ikenobo, especially its numerical aspects, may seem mysterious and esoteric to American flower arrangers who have not been previously exposed to oriental philosophy and symbolism. However, practice and application will make one's understanding of the basic philosophy of Ikenobo much easier, and will also lead the arranger more easily and naturally into the less rigorous philosophic concepts of modern schools of *Ikebana* to be presented later. After all, the concept of the positive and the negative—the "*in*" and the "*yoh*"—is not unfamiliar to the Westerner, and the philosophical idea that the present exists to illustrate the past and to presage the future, is not beyond normal human comprehension. The whole meaning of the Ikenobo style is the identification of man with nature, whether benign or malignant.

W.C.S.

The Philosophy of *Ikebana*

Human beings and plants, together with all other living things, keep their continual growth by virtue of God's blessing which envelops the entire universe. Man, from ancient times up to the present, was and still is deeply moved by looking at beautiful flowers. He holds them up for his enjoyment, and arranges them in his home to decorate it, so as to enrich his daily life. Here is *Ikebana*, then, when one feels an impulse to look at these beautiful flowers near around him.

Our ancestors, however, had long led their lives together with birds and beasts amidst the beautiful, successive alternation of the seasons; they regarded singing of birds and growling of beasts either as natural longing for companions or calling for the other sex; they also felt sympathy toward the hills and waters, grasses and trees, for the latter were equally looked upon as the same living things. Birds sing, flowers bloom, even a rolling pebble, according to our hopeful legend, is imagined to grow up into a huge mossy rock. From such a view of the life and the world, the blessing of the Gods is thought to be poured upon everything on earth, continual growth and alternation brought forth under the mercy of the Gods, and even the difficulties we sometime suffer are considered as divine tests imposed upon us. When we observe our surroundings with the thought that regards the will toward growth as the subject proper, the paved way to *Ikebana* appears.

Enduring rain and dew, and struggling against the wind and snow, plants accomplish their continuous change of themselves, while they send out buds, stretch forth new branches, and let themselves bloom in proper season, respectively.

And yet flowers bloom only for a moment, then let themselves be blown off directly after. Plants have such a destiny that they are on the one hand firmly rooted in the earth, without freedom to move about, while on the other hand they are simple but energetic in their effort to survive, and most sensitive to the blessings of nature. Even in the posture of a single flower, the foundation of creation, with all its variation, can be traced.

Here lies the foundation of Japanese *Ikebana,* where one catches deep insight through these structures of nature itself.

Ikebana does not merely aim to arrange flowers into a certain form; it aims rather to grasp the configuration of the vividly growing elastic force of plants, representing our earnest human desire to come in contact with the foundation of the creative power, through various floral arrangements. Analogically speaking, it does not attempt to admire a "waxen mannequin" as the beauty, but the basic fact itself of the "breathing human being" is the object.

By arranging flowers—when written in Japanese ideographs, this phrase means "to make flowers live"—or by looking at the figures of arranged flowers, we can listen to the words of the Gods. *Ikebana* has thus become more and more evolved, rendering both the arrangers and the spectators to keep themselves as elegant as blooming flowers and displaying the art as the act of wishing the Gods' blessing on others also.

CONCEPTS

Beginning with the first acknowledgment of the vital force of plants, and then, through this knowledge, realizing the principle which produces this force, that is to say, the creative original element that makes the universe, *Ikebana* is

formed into some suitable shape that displays it. An old saying, namely, "to know the act leads one to understand its subject," precisely points to this whole matter, the "act" meaning the phenomenon, and the "subject," the subject proper as its substance. These states of nature are revealed even by a single flowering branch, and flower-arrangers distinguish between those forces of spontaneous growth in flowers, that is, between the features by nature, and the changes by the natural environment, calling the former the "inborn nature," the latter the "nature."

It may seem unsuitable to one who loves flowers, that an arranger often cuts off beautiful flowers or graceful branches as if without mercy, yet in fact, he only attempts to follow the mysteries of the Creative Nature, by making more clear the true features of the inborn nature of flowers.

All phenomena in this world are not necessarily gratifying, yet both human beings and plants are always favored with the blessing of the Gods, and together endeavor to construct a peaceful and satisfying world. The forms of *Ikebana*, pictured by themselves, give such ideal images full of the Gods' blessings; the forms of plants inserted in flower-vessels provide ideal images through their spiritual force which penetrates to the broader space behind the present visible shapes. The rules and techniques of *Ikebana* have been introduced into our art in such a way that this visible form can be considered "the positive"—*yoh,* and the invisible one "the negative"—*in.* The two elements mutually intermingle sometimes repulsing, sometimes attracting each other, to such effect that a new universe is *re*-produced.

STRUCTURE

What *Ikebana* seeks to represent is the character of plants which do grow up, in other words, the effort of plants pursuing the ideal. To arrange flowers, "to make flowers live," in Japanese implies to find out the fundamental that constitutes the manner of growth, and to figure out the final ideal, just as in the natural action of flowering branches. The force constituting this elemental nature comes to be revealed, it is considered, as based upon the interaction of two antagonistic forces; one is the negative, the other the positive. Human beings live their lives on the borderline of life and death, tracing the path of destiny between light and darkness. Life is the positive, death is the negative. The positive is the force appearing on the surface, and the negative is that hidden

Ikebana cannot literally express the passage of time, as a dramatic performance can, but, grasping a cross-section of it at this moment, tries to represent it. For instance, by comparing a flower in full bloom with one that is just going to bloom, all shades of flower petals give us the actual feeling toward vividly growing things. Also, difference of direction between a group of pine branches extending themselves upward, and another consisting of branches stretching sideways, makes the motive of the growing force, and denotes the real feature of life itself.

Betwixt any two flowers of camellias also exists the same elastic force; as well on the branchlets of a pine tree, as in the sloping line of sidelong spreading flowers, a force to extend still farther is revealed uniformly.

inside. These contrasting forces, somewhat like the two electrical poles, are incessantly in motion, the positive turning into the negative, and vice versa. From an invisible microcosm up to the universal macrocosm, every phenomenon depends on the combination of these two forces.

Life appears in a bud, where the negative turns into the positive; the latter taking active part is filled with fresh energy, flowers then bloom, inviting butterflies, calling for insects, and, in the end, the positive turns into the negative again, leaving behind seeds that will make new development; that is to say, "the positive turns into the negative," to wait for the next spring. Thus the alternation of the negative and the positive is repeated forever, where melodies of life are heard and the rise and fall of function in general is developed. Such is the heart of a flower-arranger, who seeks the youthful extension thus revealed— the lively growth, healthy stretch, mild brightness, brightening joy, graceful loneliness, and modesty with which the plants wait for the coming spring. A ' thus again is maintained man's attitude to believe in the possibilities contained in the concept of "future," and to trust himself to the strength and will of life. This means that, while

obeying the law of "the negative and the positive," it is possible for "a man" to become the subject before he was aware, and thus participating in the creation of the universe. Identifying "the positive" with heaven, "the negative" with earth, "the man" constitutes in some sense the center of creation by following after "the heaven and earth," being himself situated between the two.

An elemental concept existed in the beginning, which developed into "the two," "the negative and the positive," and to these "the man" added to make "the three." Such is the structure of *Ikebana*. But *Ikebana* cannot express the passage of time in its phenomena. We cannot expect plants in a vase to grow up and to change by themselves.

Ikebana comes into existence by catching the endless current of life itself at one single moment. By appearing to suspend the act of eternal life, the will and joy toward growth can be felt and comprehended, and for this purpose the arrangement of flowers must be in such a way as to create an organic combination in which they can indicate the past, or suggest the future, respectively.

Fundamental Form
of *Ikebana*

POSTURE

Ikebana displays a world of the beautiful,
which is selected. It looks just as it is in
nature, yet further, complying with the
human heart, it speaks directly to us.

Great influence over the form of *Ikebana* is
determined by what sort of beauty the arranger
has in mind. It has already been stated that in the
beginning one original element first appears,
which then diverges into two, *in* and *yoh*. When
these two, *in* and *yoh*, are in perfect balance, each
having an equal strength, the form cannot display
a motion implied interiorly. In contrast, when
this balance is suspended, then generation and
development can be expected, and some possibilities contained in the "future" may appear.

We suggest that the "growing" figure makes a
distortion, and when this idea is combined with
that of shunning the balance of *in* and *yoh*, re-
specting the form of *Ikebana*, importance is
attached to the interior balance, as different from
the apparent balance.

The overflowing energy of *yoh* represents a
spring of prosperity and the development of a
hopeful future so that the selection of plant material is tried from just this standpoint and the

form of *Ikebana* is determined at the same time.

Going deeper into this same matter, we find
that when feeling the beauty in the overflowing
energy of *yoh*, everyone differs concerning the
stage where he discovers beauty, each according
to his individual sense. This difference has resulted historically in various forms of *Ikebana*,
and in the development of several schools of this
art. Comparing the rise and fall of *in-yoh* alle-
gorically with the pendulum-movement right and
left, we can understand that there exists one
school which sees beauty in the state of a pendulum that has just begun to move from right to
left, another which takes up the moment that the
pendulum touches the extreme left and still another, the moment that the pendulum just begins
to turn back to the right. Analogically speaking
again, *Ikebana* of the Ikenobo School takes the
standpoint that one sees beauty before and until
the pendulum comes up to the center line, not at
the center line itself. Speaking of flowering plants,

an artist arranges flowers from such a standpoint that he discovers beauty in the bud just going to spring forth, in the fresh branches and leaves just going to stretch themselves forth, in the flowers just going to open. Even when he arranges two flowers side by side, he attaches more importance in his representation to the bud than to the open one. When he adds dry grass to a green branch, more weight is thus given to the figure of the green branch. The past exists in order to denote the passage of time up to the present, and the present exists to presage the future.

But when we try to represent such spiritual concepts, it must be understood that this balance of *in* and *yoh* cannot be weighed quantitatively. It is therefore important to read in one's mind the interior force respectively implied. It is most important to be mentioned that, though a bud is smaller than an open flower, the former shows the more lively energy, and the green branch, though less in quantity than the dry grass, is not what is withering away, namely, it is what expresses the vital force of "will to shoot out."

This nature of things then determines the direction, the length, the order, and the strength each possesses; of the three branches corresponding to "heaven," "earth," and "man," respectively. Therefore, such techniques become necessary either to bend or cut off branches, or to thin out leaves, all of which signifies the need to follow the mysteries of Nature.

In other words, *Ikebana* of the Ikenobo esteems *beauty* in form, *the pure* in color, and tries to represent them in the posture of *Ikebana, just as they are.*

Drawing up *the genuine* from the depth of the earth, *Ikebana* of the Ikenobo tries best to create *the pure* and *the novel,* perhaps in a manner to suit the Providence of the Gods.

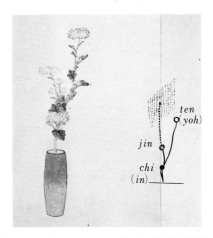

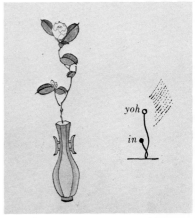

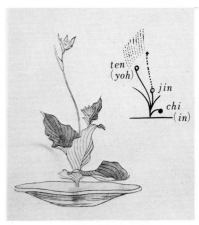

BASIC STRUCTURE

Following their surroundings, plants are not deprived of self-supporting force. They strike root deep into the earth, and spread leaves and branches toward light. There we find a life which exerts its utmost to live on, amidst rigorous surroundings. Here something is seen without being looked at, something that strikes the human heart without seeking to be looked at.

Ikebana is basically only the transferring of "the will toward growth," possessed by plants themselves, to a flower arrangement.

Accordingly, instead of just admiring the flowers themselves as beautiful in color or form, the one who arranges flowers enjoys them as beautiful just as they exist, combined with their stems and leaves. A flower-arranger considers those flowers as beautiful that are striving to live in their natural surroundings; he then tries to transfer their natural state to a flower-vase.

But it is impossible to remove the living flowers just as they are from the natural world to a flower-vase; a single branch removed as it is to a flower-vase cannot necessarily reproduce the natural beauty which it possessed in the natural landscape. Flowers on a cut-off branch, being separated from the mother earth or the environment, are deprived of their vigor; sometimes it goes so far that a shabby branch stretches itself, withering away with the leaves turned upside down. In order to keep the lively appearance of plants as they are in nature, a force substituting for that of either the earth or the principal stem must be added artificially, so as to reproduce an atmosphere in which a few branches were situated on a bush, just as here in the flower-vase.

The essential point in which *Ikebana* differs from other creative arts is that its materials are the living flowers which themselves possess speeds and directions of growth, so that one should not determine the form solely by the apparent harmony or stability.

It is generally considered that stability is important to aesthetic form, yet stability in *Ikebana* signifies a special form. Broadly speaking, something is stabilized when it keeps its balance by itself or is supported by another, without falling or tumbling down; the horizontal line against gravity therefore is here assumed. Every plant growing on the earth, however, possesses such force to rise upward by itself that it tries to stabilize the surroundings inclusive of itself. Since *Ikebana* tries to represent this growing force, instead of regarding its materials as mere matter, we must assume that this force is still active even

after flowers are arranged in a vase. When this concept is realized in the figure, plants become properly arranged—that is, *made to live* in Japanese—instead of being merely arranged.

For this purpose, a flower-vase must not be a mere vessel, but it may sometimes symbolize the mother earth, or sometimes take the part of the principal stem. Further, it sometimes represents a precipice, sometimes the surface of a pond. The material—plants assume postures to stretch themselves up, taking the vase as the cardinal point, and to rise up even higher with an elastic force. Here the branches of plants display the surroundings of the earth when rising above the vase; they show changes corresponding to their surroundings in the atmosphere when extending themselves higher, and finally express their innate nature—*the will*—at the top of the arranged branches. The strength and weakness of the strain and change suggests the surroundings, brings about the atmosphere, and projects an ideal image cherished by the artist. This is a general and fundamental posture, as each of the three branches has its own role, "the branch of earth" (*tai* the body), "the branch of heaven" (*soe* the complement), and "the branch of man" (*shin* the substance), together making up the form of *Ikebana*. (Explanations concerning "heaven," "earth" and "man" as well as "the negative and the positive" will be described once more in a later paragraph.)

When these branches, each having its size great or small, force strong or weak, growth swift or slow, direction hither or thither, are unified into one by the upward growing *will* toward light, they represent beautiful stability and harmony. Flowers thus arranged strike the hearts of the spectators most impressively.

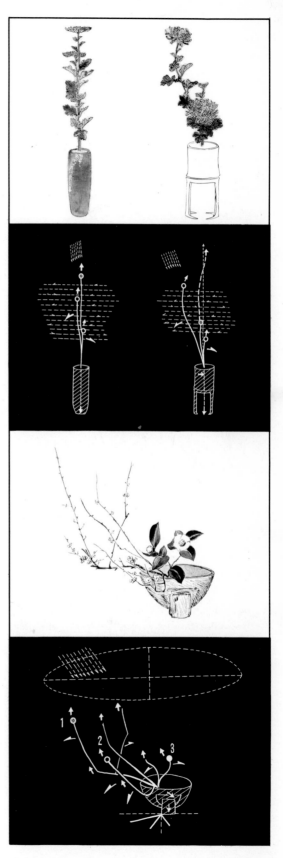

PROPORTIONS

When one arranges flowers, he can determine the length and width of branches, the size, the tone of color or of light and shade, of material flowers only by knowing what strength each part has in the whole, and in what form it is united to the whole.

It has been already stated that there are three principal parts in the ordinary form of *Ikebana*. They are, first, the branch of "the earth," having the nature of *in* (the negative) and displaying the influence of the earth; second, the branch of "the heaven," having the nature of *yoh* (the positive) and displaying in broader expression the influence of the atmosphere; and third, the branch of "the man" (*jin*) having the nature of *yoh*, too, displaying the very nature of the materials themselves, in other words, the beauty selected by the arranger himself. Of these three, the branch of the earth takes the active form in the lower part, the

branch of the heaven in the upper part, and the branch of the man, expressing the strength of intention, still higher at the uppermost part.

The branch of the man, therefore, occupying the larger space of action, is called *shin* (the true and the central) as it constitutes the central point of *Ikebana*, and the branch of the heaven, acting in the space surrounding the branch of the man, sometimes combining with it and sometimes taking such a form which supplements its strength, is called *soe* (complement); and the branch of the earth, displaying its innate nature by spreading itself in the lower part, is called *tai* (body). Thus *Ikebana* of the Ikenobo School has these three branches or parts, *shin, soe* and *tai*. When we look back over the process of how the three parts have developed into their present state, we can then realize the proper proportion of their strengths.

Ikebana does not exist independently by itself, but as a link of the whole universe, each part of which is endlessly connected with another. With respect to its form, it corresponds to the heart of the man who creates, or one who looks at *Ikebana*. In like manner, each part, the individual, of *Ikebana* is linked one with another and each connected with the whole. Every respective section comes to appear as representing an incomplete form that seeks to be completed. Thus is revealed the "present" that develops, or our hope towards the "future."

It has already been stated that, where there is a phenomenon, there must be first *the elemental*, which then develops into two, *in* and *yoh*; when these two lose their balance, then "the future" may be expected. When a third force comes to act on it, the balance of *in* and *yoh* is broken, but when the third force reaches a certain level, then the two, *in* and *yoh*, come to unite into one, regaining the role of "*the elemental* in the next stage." Such is the theory in which one can assert that "one *is* two, and two *is* one," hence *in* becomes *yoh* when the point of time corresponding to the former changes considerably, and vice versa. That a third force always takes action and the whole develops into itself, can be interpreted in the abstract formula that "one becomes two, and *a new two* as a third force appearing thereto, the whole returns to *one*, then 'another two' corresponding to the former 'new two' appears to make 'the five' which constitutes a new elemental at the next stage, producing 'seven,' and further 'nine,' and so forth." Such a relation of develop-

ment is denoted by the phrase "seven-five-three," *Shichi-go-san*. The three principal branches of *Ikebana*, and the minor parts also, are constructed in such a way that they form a chain of forces. It is our principle to regard *shin* as "the seven," *soe* as "the five," and *tai* as "the three." Yet there arise differences of the form, according to the point of time when the third force is caught in the process of this development. The structure of *Ikebana* is always accompanied by invisible forces, just as when one sees the crescent moon that is *partly concealed*. It is important to make the structure of *Ikebana* keep in itself an expectation that such a force will appear just as when the waxing moon will become the full moon. For a man who looks at *Ikebana*, it is also equally important that he should assume an attitude that tries to fill in those phenomena *incomplete* or *concealed* in appearance. This may be said of the characteristic feature of Japanese traditional arts in general, not of *Ikebana* alone.

RIKKA

As to the forms of *Ikebana, rikka* was the first to be established. In the first half of the 17th century, assemblies for flower arrangement under the supervision of Ikenobo Senko were held at various places, beginning with the Imperial court, at the mansions of nobility, or at shrines and temples. Many pictures of *rikka* arranged by Senko remain to this day, which show us the forms of *Ikebana* at that period.

52

This photograph shows a *rikka* arranged, according to the manner of Senko, on the alcove of *Oko-zashiki* (minor room where profound instruction of *tanka* poetry to the Emperors, and the like, were performed in old days when Their Majesties resided in Kyoto) of Kyoto Gosho (Imperial residence). This masterpiece, combined with a picture of a distant mountain ranges at its back, gives us an impression of wonderful scenic interest.

NAGEIREBANA

(thrown-in form of old times)

While *rikka* gradually acquired a fixed form and after a long prosperous period finally descended to mannerism, there arose a tendency toward trying to arrange flowers and plants plainly, just as they *act* in nature. The result was that, at the beginning of the 18th century, *nageirebana* became popular. Then, along with the new attention to the life energy of plants, *nageirebana* gradually developed into *shoka* form.

These photographs show a work arranged on the alcove of the tearoom "*chosetsu*"—*listening to snow*—in Kyoto Gosho, according to the manner of about the middle of the 18th century, using plums and camellias as flower materials, and a bamboo vessel with two side-openings (*nijugiri*) as the flower-vase.

Nageirebana used to be arranged originally before the rikka form was established. While rikka shows scenic and formative interest, complying with ceremonial requirements, nageirebana on the contrary came into being from the original concept of Ikebana that its object lies in admiring the very flowers themselves, and at the same time it tries to realize spiritual communication between the arranger and the spectators. Accordingly, nageirebana has been arranged in various forms—erected form, thrown-in form, bent form, hung-down form—in accordance with the character of the plants used. Also, in accordance with the shape of the vessel used, appropriate forms such as okihana (laid Ikebana), kakehana (hung Ikebana), and tsurihana (hung-down Ikebana), could be selected, and further, in accordance with either the place where the flowers were arranged, the sort of annual observances celebrated, or the interests of the visitors expected, sometimes literary and sometimes artistic devices were used and the superior intelligence that quite fitted the design to the respective case has been highly esteemed.

This photograph shows a composition with a narrow-mouthed vase in which stems of pampas-grass and corn flowers (Lychnis) are arranged. A sign of autumn stealing in from the outside window is deepened by the wind-blown nature of the pampas-grass together with the lonely cinnabar color reflected by the corn flowers. The white back of the sliding paper window, with its lineal lattices, combine to give the whole display a highly artistic beauty.

Among the various *nageirebana* forms, the *tsuribana* (hung-down *Ikebana*) has received special attention. Boat-shaped vessels have been devised representing, for instance, the boats sailing in and out of harbors, that symbolize the happy development of society, in order to seek variations in design.

This photograph shows a composition of a basket-shaped vase hung in a lineal architectural pattern with the plants arranged in it so that they present soft curves, make contrasts of brightness and darkness, or curves and straight lines. It is made even more impressive with the addition of chrysanthemum flowers attached to the Eulalia-grass, and corresponding with the design of the *Jibukuro* (cupboard in the lower part). All these contrasts, interrelating with one another, emphasize the actual nature of life itself.

SHOKA

As interest rose in the inherent beauty of the entire structure of a bundle of grass or a tree, *nageirebana* came to a fixed form under the name of *shoka* in the beginning of the 19th Century

This photograph shows a form of *kakehana* (hung-down style) of *shoka* from *Ikebana*, side-hanging in this case, where spiraea branches and a rose of Sharon are arranged in a vase of bamboo pipe, the whole representing in *shoka* form the natural shape of the material plants just as they are, following their own nature.

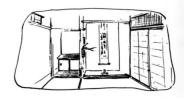

NAGEIRE

(thrown-in style of the modern age)

Along with the prospering of the *shoka* form, the basic principle became more important than the individual quality of material plants, and its form gradually acquired a standardized tendency, and about the beginning of the present century, *Ikebana* of the primitive period with simple vitality came to attract general attention, and thus arose the *nageire-moribana* style, which corresponds to our present living environment and to floricultural development.

This photograph shows an *Ikebana* of gentian together with Eulalia-grass arranged in a narrow-mouthed vase of celadon porcelain, put on a shelf board of a simplified alcove. The arranger tried to simplify the structure, utilizing the vacant space, so as to create a refreshing atmosphere.

MORIBANA (heaped-up flowers)

Moribana style gained its name from the original fact that it was arranged in a basin as if flowers were heaped up. In the early stage of *nageirebana* there was already such a heaped up form for an *Ikebana* to put on a shelf, yet we can say that it was rarely done except for displaying a work of special intention, because of the slow development of *hanadome* (flower fasteners). Since new sorts of *hanadome*—especially the *kenzan* (needle-point holder, literally meaning sword-mountains)—were contrived, *moribana* has come to occupy an important position in *Ikebana*.

This photograph shows an *Ikebana* of Japanese iris arranged in a vase of special shape, with the intention of compacting the complicated structure of the alcove, in order to represent the refreshing early summer.

Development of Creative Representation

Since the end of World War II, along with the increase of cultural intercourse between Japan and the other countries of the world, innovative evolutionary development has been introduced into *Ikebana* also. While *Ikebana* of the former days had represented the arranger's feeling indirectly, by entrusting it to the nature of the plants and trees, that of the present Ikenobo has altered its tendency toward a more direct expression of the arranger's feeling, through his creative work. It tries to express ever more directly the feeling and intention of the arranger himself, by means either of stimuli received from the figures, colors, and the qualities of material objects, or of the internal repletion of sculptural composition, and so forth.

This photograph shows an *Ikebana* of Indian-lotus fruits together with camellia flowers arranged in a highly fired pottery vase. It is set in a successful balance between the interest as a creative work and the characteristics as an *Ikebana*.

Styles of *Ikebana*

NAGEIRE

The historical development of *Ikebana* extending over four centuries is nothing but the history of Ikenobo itself. The three forms, *rikka, shoka,* and *nageire-moribana*, are still used prevailingly today and, further, they are going to bring forth the "formative" development.

Of all the forms of *Ikebana, nageire* is the most easily managed, by which we can fully appreciate the beauty of flowers and leaves. Furthermore, as the large space where branches and leaves are in action enables the work to project the nature of plants more easily, this form is now the most popular. This photograph shows an arrangement, most representative of the *nageire* form, which displays brilliant beauty revealed in simplicity. The combination of green pine branches, the vase of blue glaze, and two pink roses with deep green leaves at their back, displays brilliantly the most vivid life. (See p. 66)

MORIBANA

This photograph illustrates one of the most representative styles of the *moribana* form. Here hydrangeas, together with leaves of *Iris japonica,* are arranged in a ponderous pottery basin of compote-shape. An effort was made to represent the color transition from pink to purple, as well as the vigorous freshness of hydrangeas. Between the two factors, namely, the hanging inclination of the hydrangeas and the contrasting force trying to pull it back, possessed by the pointed leaf-edges of the Japanese iris, there is revealed a moderate tension in the balance of the two forces, which makes this vivid freshness of hydrangeas most impressive. Also the equalized mass of hydrangea flowers shows the most beautiful balance held by the three main parts, *shin, soe* and *tai,* accented by the unbalanced leaves of Japanese iris.

SHOKA

Shoka is an *Ikebana* form in which one tries to find out the basic source of life's energy and to represent its pure and earnest force in a simple figure. While showing the force of will, born of the earth, at the water's edge where the stem of *Ikebana* separates from the flower-vessel, it stretches up, drawing mild arc lines, and shows delicate response to the surroundings, so as to represent its own will amidst the sharp correspondence of the three main branches, *shin, soe,* and *tai,* with one another.

This photograph shows an example of the most exact and rigid form of *shoka,* in which two sorts of chrysanthemums, large-flowered and small-flowered, are arranged in a copper vessel, representing the most beautiful quality of chrysanthemums.

RIKKA

As for *rikka*, the entire complex shape being composed of seven or nine principal parts, it befits compositions expressing scenic interest. (See the explanation on p. 112)

64

NAGEIRE

As for its shape, *nageire* may adopt the standing style, the slanting style, the waving style, and the hanging-down style, etc. In the *nageire* of Ikenobo, the standing style is called *chokutai* (the erect state), which is quite suitable for expressing simple atmosphere or the sublime mood. This photograph shows a composition of peach twigs and daffodils arranged in a pottery vessel with comb-shaped deep notches. The arranger tried to make the materials also express soft curved lines as if they enclosed the space, just reflecting ample influence of the outline curves of this vessel. This sort of *nageire* may suggest to one's mind the warm sunbeams of a bright spring field.

Methods of Arranging *Nageire*

The order of treatment is as follows:

1. To select the materials; to determine the direction of the vessel; to cleanse the leaves of dirt;

2. To determine the direction, the slant, and the length of the pine branch; to affix it to the vessel by binding a prop to the root;

3. To arrange rose flowers, adjusting the direction of the flowers and cutting off unsuitable leaves.

①

③

②

When you arrange *Ikebana*, first take up the plants and cut off all the dirty, withered or dead parts, observing carefully each branch, one by one, from various points of view. Determine in your mind the concept to be represented by your arrangement, and decide the outline of the composition and the vessel to be used, after studying the posture of the plants.

When these preparations are finished, the branch selected for the main part should be put in good condition by scissoring off surplus twigs or such parts that seem to interfere with the interesting shape of other branches, sparing no attachment to the materials. Such a forceful branch should be the *shin*, fit to constitute the principal axis of the work, and another branch, having a force secondary to the *shin* and fit to respond to it, should be the *soe*, and another such one, though rather short in length but possessing a force capable of reinforcing the entire figure, should be the *tai*.

Then, after the composition is thus decided, insert the first branch, complying with the shape of the vessel, into the vase. In order to fix it tightly in the vase, shapes with less compulsion are preferred, but where fixing is difficult by reason of the present composition, you can either set a prop at the vase-mouth, bend the root of materials, or bind a supporting piece of wood to them. Next insert the second branch in accordance with the inclination of the first one. By inserting the second branch, the intention of the composed work becomes clearer, but in the case where there lies a certain compulsion in the composed figure, you should insert the third branch, adding suitable amendments. The fixing method is just as in the first branch. If the first branch is inserted toward the right, the second should lean toward the left; if the former is faced forward, then the latter should face backward. Insert one branch after another alternately, according to the order of hardness or easiness of the insertion techniques, keeping in mind that the work as a whole should incline forward as if it is calling to those who see it.

These photographs show a composition in which the arranger has attempted to emphasize the balanced beauty of pink roses with green leaves at their back, and notwithstanding the usual custom that pine branches are to be inserted aslant, the present one is stretched out sideways corresponding with the sidelong extension of the vessel. Although this intention cannot be said to correspond effectively to the innate nature of pine trees, such exceptional treatment has been made because of the principal intention of expressing the beauty of the roses, and this very procedure proved very successful in reproducing the vivid appearance of the roses.

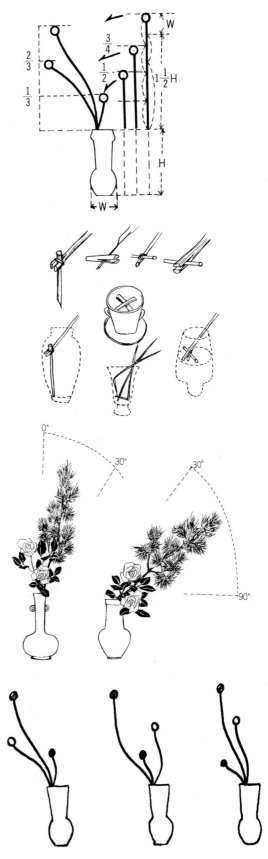

These photographs show a work in which a *Cypripedium* orchid has been arranged in a pottery vessel without special technique, that is, by merely inserting the flower into the vase and letting it keep its natural slant. Such a slanting form is called *shatai* (the slant state). It can be most easily arranged and is the most suitable for representing simple and intimate feelings.

Appropriate to the natural habit of *Cypripedium* to bloom facing downward, the flower in this work allows the noble beauty in the simple shape to overflow into its surroundings. How the leaves are disposed in their position is just as important as how much the flower is to be slanted. It was so arranged that its posture makes us feel as if the long leaf, belonging to the *soe* and embracing the flower, flows out according to its natural tendency. The expression of the flower becomes vivid; and the short leaf belonging to the *tai*, by facing rather upward close to the flower-stalk so as to supplement the weakness of the latter, suggests to our mind the vital impetus of living flowers.

In order to enhance the effect of this *Ikebana*, the structure of the window was taken into account. The lines of the arranged *Cypripedium* are projected in strong relief by the back lighting, while those lines of the window that are active in a perpendicular direction supplement the apparent weakness of the flower-vessel, adding a phase of stability to the large-headed flower shape.

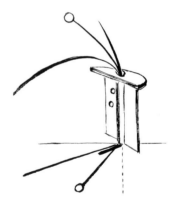

The arranger tried to avoid the defect that the flower shape might become flattened, by rendering the respective direction of the flower and the two leaves different from the direction the tips point to, so that the flower shape, enclosing a large space, makes us feel a long depth to the work. But it is important that the work as a whole slants forward and "calls" to those who see it.

This photograph shows a composition of a single rose flower placed together with broomcorn and arranged in a pot of *sake*-bottle shape. Inserting two or three kinds of materials together is intended to make the meaning of the represented object clearly impressive to the spectators. By adding broomcorn to the rose, the autumnal season becomes tangible to us. Though the core of the present representation lies in the beauty of the rose, spectators can also sense the beauty of autumn by the annexed broomcorn, according to their own respective experience.

When two or more materials are arranged together, it is necessary that, in spite of some characteristic points common to them, there should be marked contrasts among other factors. If the season and the environment of the growing land are equal, then the more the shape, color or quality varies, the more contrasting beauty can be seen, enabling the principal object to be enhanced. In like manner, when one shape is similar to another, then the colors and qualities should be different, and when the colors are similar, then those materials whose shapes and qualities are different should be placed together. As is shown in the photograph, it is because we have common sensibility that the autumnal mood tends to be deepened by annexation of broomcorns, and the impressive beauty of the rose is doubly emphasized by this contrast of characters.

That cut flowers look "alive" in a flower-vessel is because once separated branches cut from plants are restored to the same order.they possessed while living in nature, they realize in the flower-vessel a new environment. It is most important, speaking from the arranger's standpoint, that he should reconstruct the same order in a new environment as the plants possessed in their natural state. For this purpose, attention must be given to the place where spectators stand and to the direction of light upon the work.

When we look at flowers growing in nature, we see their most beautiful sides, those parts of the flowering plants which generally receive the most abundant light pouring out usually either from just the upper side of the spectator's back, or from somewhere just right or left of the upper side.

Flowering plants stretch their branches, spread their leaves, and open their blossoms toward this light. Also, the stems and roots keep resisting against it so as to maintain this inclination. Taking these relations into account in *Ikebana*, the arranger tries to set the unifying point on the right or left upper back-side of the spectators, and endeavors to keep a beautiful balance between the weighty appearance of the vessel and the impetus of the parts which have branches and leaves that tend to stretch themselves toward the back of the *Ikebana*.

Each of the two works reproduced on these facing pages is an *Ikebana* in which the tendency of plants to stretch toward light is impressively felt. For this purpose, the unifying point has been imaginarily set in a rather lower position than is usual, the slanting degree of the flower shape being determined markedly greater.

The *Ikebana* on the opposite page is so arranged that the chrysanthemums and the Eulalia-grass have been given such a frank directionality*—pointing to something—and while the chrysanthemum flowers have been made to look predominant because of separation from the white-glazed bottle by adding gerbera leaves at their back, stabilization of flower shape has also been attempted.

The *Ikebana* above is a work of *Nandina* and *Narcissi* which represents, while showing in itself gentle curves in antipodal contrast to the former, the strong tendency of pointing to something by repeating the curves of three long leaves following after the *Narcissi* blades that run to the right.

Here we find mild movement as well as broad space. The choice between these two works de-

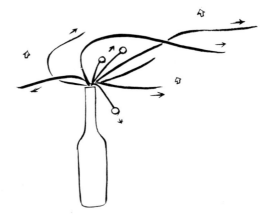

pends on the seasonal distinction of spring and autumn, and also on consideration of the environment created in a room decorated with such a work.

* Here the present translator proposes to introduce a new technical term *directionality*.

This photograph shows a work of hydrangea mixed with common reed, and arranged in a green-glazed bottle placed on a shelf well above the floor, on the side of an alcove. Those *Ikebana* designed to decorate a higher place should be finished up with a wind-blown or a hung-down shape. It is usual to use materials for them that naturally bend or hang, but in the present work the arranger has altered the visual quality of the materials by splitting the blades of the reeds lengthwise along their veins so as to satisfy his creative requirement. So to speak, a sort of fiction has been performed and, indeed, looking at this work, we are compelled to imagine that such a state of things can really exist. Besides, when we look at these reddish-purple flowers of hydrangea through the splits of the blades, the beauty of hydrangeas as the principal object becomes even more impressive. This kind of style in which the position is lower than the insertion opening of a flower-vessel is called *suitai* (the hung-down state).

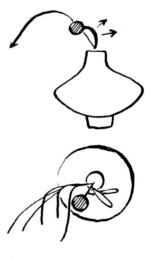

The *Ikebana* with which a room is decorated may have various styles, depending on the construction of the house. This photograph shows a work of *Hototogisu* (a kind of wild herb, *Tricyrtis hirta* Hook. var. *parviflora* Masamune), and gladiolus leaves arranged together in a bamboo-pipe vessel with a single side-opening (*ichijugiri*) hung on a pillar, finished in the hanging style (*kakebana*) by way of the *nageire* form. The beautiful view seen outside the window plays the part of the background in this composition, but, generally speaking, the Japanese *Ikebana* does not stand in opposition to "Nature," but is arranged as a work which always follows natural scenes, or which is conscious of being a part of nature in itself, even when it is interrupted by a wall or a paper-slide. The lonesome beauty of *Hototogisu* suitable to the bamboo vessel puts us in an autumnal mood, and yet, just at the point where this loneliness, the subject itself being supported by a single level line of the sharp cut side-opening of the bamboo vessel, and by the toughness of the gladiolus leaves, shows at the top end of their stems an impetus of living things, *there* this work is filled with a deep impressive yearning for human life.

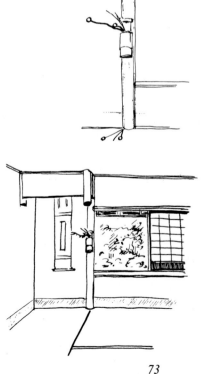

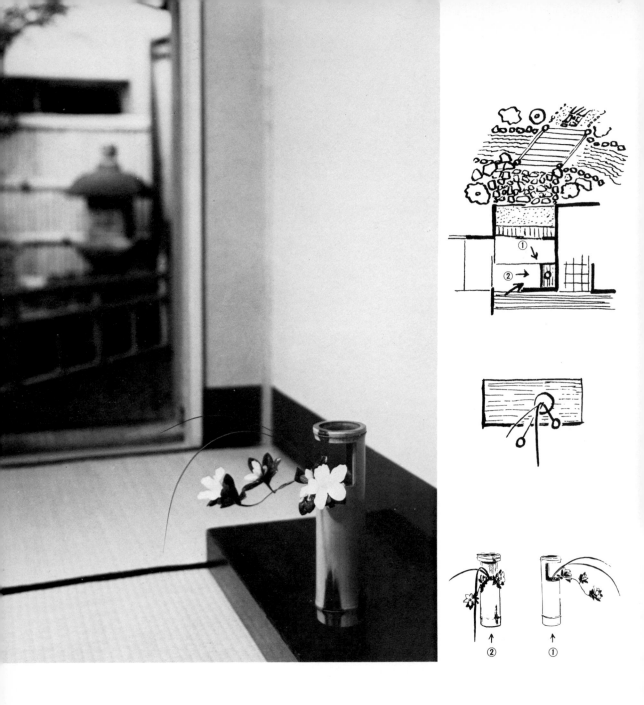

This photograph shows a *nageire* decorating a corner of the entrance in a dwelling. Here, small branches of azaleas together with *Acorus* are arranged in an *ichijugiri* or bamboo vessel, set on the *Okidoko* (a simplified alcove installed only with a flat wooden stand laid on the mat). *Ikebana* arranged for decorating the entrance gives the first impression to a visitor, but the place where he appreciates the work may change. So it is necessary that, though the figure is seen mainly from the direct front entrance, the figure may also be seen from the back and should be finished up as a well-ordered shape. Therefore it has been the traditional attitude of the Japanese to arrange flowers in a chaste, modest and brief manner.

Though the flower shape can be well adjusted by using azalea only—one of these two materials —the arranger, taking into consideration the characteristics of the *Ikebana* placed in the entrance, tried to give extension and depth to the flower form by adding leaves of morrow sedge.

This photograph shows the figure seen from the back, but when it is viewed directly from the front, from the entry, the flowers on the branch-top lengthily stretch forward, and lean their heads toward appreciative spectators.

MORIBANA

Moribana, which holds the principal position in the *Ikebana* of modern age, does not differ substantially from *nageire*, only showing a certain difference in the techniques of fixing flower branches according to the respective shape of vessels. Furthermore, as wide-mouthed vessels are employed in *moribana*, a large space can be embraced by the figure of a work, and in the course of time, it has come to part with the original piling-up shape, differentiating into the standing shape, the slanting shape, the bending shape, and the hanging shape, so as to enable the arranger to represent all sorts of signifying contents, according to both the born nature of plants and the intention of the arranger. *Ikebana* of the creative composition newly appeared has developed into a fashionable one, being based also upon those techniques of *moribana*.

This photograph shows a composition of calla lily, a leaf of *Fatsia japonica*, and leaves of Japanese iris arranged together in a square glass dish.

The slanting figure of the leaf of *Fatsia japonica*, and the curved lines of the leaves of Japanese iris, bending toward the former as if the latter followed after them, look so exceedingly relaxed that one who looks at the work will perceive wide and calm space encircled by them. The strong impressiveness of the snow-white flower of calla lily facing to the left gives elasticity to the materials facing to the right, by which the arranger has aimed at the special balance fit to *Ikebana*.

Methods of Arranging *Moribana*

The piling-up form, if arranged just as the name literally means, will become the kind of assortment of materials piled up in a dish that used to be seen in a still life, because flowers for it either laid lengthwise, or only the flower-heads are piled up, and the short flower-stalks or stems are kept out of sight. But plants are, for the most part, possessed of stems and they *grow*, stretching up from the earth. So long as *Ikebana*, therefore, is intended to represent the function of plants that always endeavor to accomplish their growth, such a method is apt to result in neglecting the real nature of the materials. According ly, while *moribana* depicts the nature of plants by dealing with flower-stalks proportionally longer on one hand, it also shows interest in the combination of colors and qualities or the like on the other. The methods of its representation and composition are almost the same as those of *nageire*, and a *kenzan* is still used today for fixing flower-stalks.

These photographs show the juniper, small flowers of chrysanthemum, together with leaves of *Iris japonica* arranged in a pottery vessel with a brim having open-work. First of all, materials are selected and the same preparatory operations as in *nageire* are then completed.

Then the arranger submerges a *kenzan* into the bottom of the vessel, and, cutting the lower end of juniper back to the proper length, he inserts the bent end between the needles of the *kenzan* in order to let it lean on the vessel. Next he inserts two or three small chrysanthemum flowers on the *kenzan*, making them slant deeply foward, in order to be moderately connected with the vessel. There remains now, between the juniper and the vessel, an interval that is *not* touching yet not parting with each other. A few more chrysanthemum flowers are inserted behind, slanted forward, and arranged so as to make a group of the small flowers and add bright coloring to the juniper. At that time unnecessary surplus branches and flowers should be scissored off for the sake of beautiful disposition, so as to keep these two material groups in a proper balance of volume. Yet these two materials alone are not enough to occupy ample space suitable for living figures, so that the arranger adds blades of *Iris japonica* that overspread with large curves above the juniper, in order to

partition an adequate portion out of the space. By this handling the juniper as well as small chrysanthemums become capable to represent lively expression, by dint of background newly given for growing up, that is to say, these three—*Iris japonica*, juniper, and small chrysanthemums—as a whole have built up a microcosm, and each part is bestowed with its own respective force and function corresponding to the *shin,* the *soe,* and the *tai.*

How to Use the *Kenzan*

When inserting a branch in a *kenzan,* do so slowly, taking in hand the lowest part of the branch.

Try not to force it *into* the needles, but rather to fit it *between* them.

The lower end of a branch should necessarily be cut off obliquely, and small slits are to be made with scissors.

When inserting obliquely, determine the facing and direction of the branch by inserting it for trial in a *kenzan,* and cut off an end obliquely, retaining the side to be slanted which is given cut slits, and after it is inserted first perpendicularly, slant it gradually.

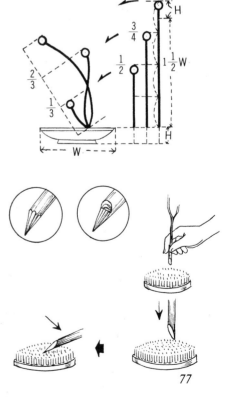

These photographs show a work which should be classified into the *nageire* form, but the author has reproduced it here rather as a *moribana*, for the reason that its atmosphere, in which autumnal flower plants are piled up in a basket, shows the quality of a *moribana*. Also, the flower stems have been fixed in a *kenzan* and a bamboo pipe has been placed in the basket in order to preserve water for the inserted flowers.

In this work, Eulalia-grass, patrinia, chinese bell-flower and small-flowered chrysanthemums are arranged together, each of which contrasts in shape and color with the other, yet representing a beautiful sight of autumnal plants in which each one brings the others to life in mutual co-operation. This is because various materials suggest an intimacy among themselves, resulting from the equality in season and environment of habitat. Furthermore, technically speaking, in point of easy composition, this bamboo basket with handle is a precisely suitable vessel, into which gathered wild plants appear in a throw-in arrangement. Suggesting to us an intimacy between the vessel and the plants as regards their quality, the arranged materials, each showing difference in length and direction with one another, also display harmonious beauty by the unified *will* toward the light thrown from the upper left side.

These photographs show a work of willow branches and daffodils, representing the throbbing joy of early spring and through this very form we can realize the quality of the space composed by *Ikebana.*

The willow branches seem to move in all directions, the curve of each branch partitioning the space in many ways, but those parts of space indicated by these lines are not solid ones, as those formed by architectural construction, but are connected with environment, and are given such a latent impetus that, once a certain pressure is given to them on one place, the whole may be expected to change organically and provoke itself to successive movement.

In the world of *Ikebana,* we characterize the respective materials and space of works as lively or lifeless, according to whether they participate in such an organic chain-combination or not. A work of *Ikebana* should be animated, the parts of which one and all interact in lively combination.

When we look at this work of *moribana* just after appreciating the former one, we can realize the solid construction produced in *Ikebana*. This photograph tells us of the interior fullness of autumn, yet which is still not a sculptural fulfilment, but has a softness like that of living things, and assumes a posture that will display the interior fullness in the movement toward the external world. The vivid color contrast shown in the combination of *Monstera*, dahlias, roses, and unicorn plants, arranged together in a cobalt-blue basin, is accompanied by refreshing feelings.

Though an *Ikebana* is regarded as an artistic work that suggests and represents the movement of living things, attention should also be called to its contrasting representation of the vegetable quietness, which in turn suggests to our mind the receptive earth, Mother of All.

An *Ikebana* is usually a work with only one side as front, but sometimes, as in the present one, it may be composed with two fronts, one on each side. On such an occasion, the arranger should be careful to consider well the background, lest the work lose its sense of vitality.

These photographs show a *moribana* composed of a Cape jasmine and leaves of *Iris japonica* arranged in a legged, square basin of green glaze. It has been arranged in a simple shape so as to fit into an abridged alcove in one corner of a small room. The whiteness of the Cape jasmine, in contrast with the green color that flows in succession from the vessel to the leaves, is most impressive.

A simple Japanese room encircled by rough walls (cob-coating or clay-wall with an unpolished surface) will have its beauty enhanced by the usual ornaments, namely, a picture or a writing and an *Ikebana* to decorate the alcove. For this purpose, *Ikebana* also needs a sort of strength in spite of its brevity. The space occupied by the side walls and the shelf becomes *living* space by putting an *Ikebana* in it.

Creative Developments in *Ikebana*

Ikebana has, by its structure, developed into an artistic work that reproduces a microcosm by the union of the *Heaven,* the *Earth,* and the *Man,* in other words, the *shin,* the *soe,* and the *tai.* Into such a work the arranger tries to imbue his impressive feelings for human life, using the living efforts of plants to this end. There are also revealed the various characteristics of the material plants, accompanied at the same time by their respective limitations.

Yet this fact comprises by itself the defect of making arrangers unable to gain the equal aesthetic experience on account of the difference in their natural environments.

Again, since life has manifold variety, the arranger becomes more inclined to discover a more direct way to represent his own complex feelings, instead of trying to give indirect expression by depending on the posture of the plant materials. *Ikebana* has thus continued to make a creative evolution more pictorial and sculptural in its character than ever.

This photograph shows a work of calla lily and bulrush inserted in a cobalt-blue compote, in which the arranger has tried to display creative beauty, while fully realizing the characteristics of *Ikebana.*

Apart from the appearance of growing things, by bending the bulrush, regarding it as plant material in order to use it as an interesting background and also regarding the conversation of the two calla lily flowers as the foreground, the arranger has endeavored to give a dramatic effect to the representation of a tasteful encounter.

This photograph shows a work of broomcorn, Italian millet (*Setaria italica*), and dahlias inserted together in white-glazed pottery showing a raw, earthen surface in which the arranger displays the interest and beauty shown by the contrasts of the respective materials, including the vessel. An autumnal mood comes out of the materials, yet without positively intending to create such an atmosphere that suggests an autumnal scene to us.

Here the arranger tried to show beautiful contrast by setting the brownish-orange area of *kibi* and *awa* stretching perpendicularly and the soft white area of the vessel spreading horizontally, against the dark red of the dahlia situated a little right of center, and also attempted to give stability to the work by setting a force flowing toward the left, against the intentionally concentrated strength of the group of dahlias.

The strong feelings commonly felt in the three materials, the vessel, *kibi* and *awa*, the feeling of soft fineness in dahlia, and the feeling received from the closely combined materials in spite of the difference in shape and color—all these unite in one body to represent the beauty that may be seen in pastel paintings.

This photograph shows a work of Cape jasmine and copse branchlets dyed coral, arranged in a vessel of light green glaze, representing an unusually bewitching beauty. There are seen coral colored branchlets spreading as if they embraced space within themselves, and white flowers of Cape jasmine encircled by mild green are glowing fragrantly *there*, *where* this spreading movement is settled up. There we find a tranquility and stillness prepared, for trusting ourselves thereto.

The scenes represented by *Ikebana* should be ones in which, even when strong motion is prevailing, just in the figure of calmly growing plants, a sign of the same can be found. The arranger has tried to produce this as a creative work of his psychological experience, in the process of which, showing the original feature in the figure of Cape jasmine, he contrasted with it the branchlets transmuted by tranquil dyeing as direct materials to express his feelings, so as to get a contrasting effect between movement and tranquility.

This photograph shows a work composed of artificial hydrangeas and bleached summer-cypress arranged in a brown-glazed vessel with projecting protuberances, to which the arranger has attempted to give creative interest in shape and color. As to the natural property of the materials, those that originally do not naturally hang down, when they are given some shape different from their own, will display visual resistance. This technique has been devised from the shape of the vessel with protuberances, and here interest in subjective construction is represented in the entire figure which consists of three elements, namely, lines flowing from the upper area to the lower, the protuberances that, like stairs, stand abreast, and the color of artificia hydrangeas grading from purple to pink as if to fill the intervals.

Ikebana for Annual and Special Observances

The third of March is the Girls' Festival. when a gorgeous set of courtly dolls, such as the Prince and His Princess accompanied by civil and military officers and lady-attendants, together with miniature furnishings and utensils, is decorated from door to door, and peach-blossoms are arranged in celebration of this festival.

Ikebana, which originated in an offering to Gods, and as an object that calls for divine blessing upon human beings, is still today arranged on every occasion whether of happy events or sorrowful affairs. Preserving an artistic nature, still *Ikebana* ought to be what belongs to the general public. One feels pleasure in the act of arranging, which inspires the arranger himself and also pleases those who look at his work.

In observing a birthday of a beloved child, at marriage, in a usual home life, or in a memorial service of one's intimate friend, flowers used to be arranged heart and soul. Furthermore, in the numerous annual observances which color the four seasons, Japanese people used to enjoy themselves by arranging flowers suitably for each occasion.

The New Year's flower arrangement: moribana *of long-leaf pine-branches and roses arranged with wishes for eternal youth and long life. It is a traditional attitude of the Japanese to mend his way on the New Year's Day. An auspicious painting or writing is to be decorated and pine, bamboo, Japanese apricot branches and the like are usually arranged in the alcove, each plant carrying with itself certain longing of human life corresponding to the respective nature.*

Flowers arranged for the Doll's Festival: peach blossoms, willow branches, and camellia flowers are arranged in kakehana style.

Flowers arranged for the moon-light party: the full moon viewed in the mid-autumn is the most beautiful sight of the moon to be expected in Japan. On that day flowers of Eulalia-grass are arranged in a posture of meeting the moon and all the family waits for the moon to come up.

The fifth of May is the Boys' Festival, when dolls of ancient sages and warriors are decorated and flowers of Japanese iris are arranged for its celebration, in which an instinct for healthy growth and great righteousness are expressed.

This photograph shows a typical work designed to celebrate a happy event, such as the completion of a new building, a change of residence, a marriage, etc.

A picture of the noted mountain, Fujiyama, which symbolizes Japan, is hung in the alcove, and a *kakehana* of pine branch and camellia decorates its pillar. Combination of the two factors, namely, the visual element showing Mt. Fuji standing high beyond and far above the pinery on the one hand, and both the auditory harmony and contents which represent *fuji* sounding "the immortal and the invariable" (evergreen needles or leaves) and meaning longevity, on the other, has become one of the traditional techniques.

In this manner, pictures or writings and *Ike-* *bana* are so selected that they have some connection with each other in their meaning, and it has become a common way to avoid such duplicated figures as a picture of flowers and an *Ikebana* of flowers.

Moreover, the form of *Ikebana* is to be adopted according to the seriousness or to the degree of importance of the occasion. Accordingly, for serious and solemn observances, rigid forms are selected.

This photograph shows a work of a simple observance, such as for receiving intimate friends, the alcove being also of abridged form. In a formal alcove, even when a *kakehana* is arranged, the side-hang form is considered to be the normal one.

The Way to the *Shoka* Form

Ikebana has repeated various phases in its historical path. Beginning with the pursuit of external beauty in flowers, entering its interior in the course of time, passing from a simple form to a complex one, pursuers of *Ikebana* realized that the fundamental elements had been born from the single principle, realizing the truth in a fiction, and discovering the invariable in the fashionable. But they did not attain it at a stroke, but have grown to possess the pure, rejecting formal vanity, after repeating apparently similar passages, from the simple to the complex. From *tatebana* (original standing form) to *rikka* (formalized standing form), and from *nageirebana* (older thrown-in form) to *shoka* (simplified form of *rikka*), and today from *nageire-moribana* (thrown-in, piled-up

form) to creative composition, the historical path of ever evolving *Ikebana* still continues.

This photograph shows a work of *moribana* in which a slender bamboo branch and red camellias are arranged in a tripodal pottery of big-lined simple shape, and the arranger has arranged in its simple composition elements akin to that of *shoka*. The path to the *shoka* form consists in adding a delicate balance of force to this form of construction.

Living plants spring from the maternal earth, spread their leaves, and bear fruit until their lives end. Sometimes composed, sometimes charming, and sometimes with refined beauty they develop in response to their respective circumstances. A flower arranger always racks his brains to find out just the proper point of time when he should take advantage of the beauty of growing plants.

The surface of the earthen vessel, hard baked in the kiln, shows the color print of fire on its surface. Its brilliant green glaze as well as the soft curves of staff vine, whose seeds and stems still remain green, give a youthful and heart-rending mood of simplicity, where a single flower of tree peony splendidly shines in contrast to the bright green.

The youthful and simple beauty represented in this *nageire* is directly connected with the sense of beauty esteemed in Ikenobo's *shoka*.

Because both flowers and men equally breathe the atmosphere and have the same relation to each other, Japanese *Ikebana* has come into existence.

The persistent sign of the contrast in plants withering away, and the approaching sign of distraction in the same, do not suggest a gloomy mood to us, but represent an expectation concerning something that is coming into the world. A plant, just as a man, being embraced in divine blessing that pervades the whole universe, accom-

plishes its growth and thus is promised to be revived. Catching this flashing moment, the arranger creates a work of *Ikebana*.

Two tassels of summer cypress stretching upward begin to show indistinctly some trend toward disturbing their co-operation in life. The gap between the two and their arched top-edges suggest these states, but by adding a scarlet hibiscus resplendently blooming, a vivid impression pointing to revival is indicated. This is a *moribana* that tends to approach *shoka* form.

This photograph shows a *moribana* of a large chrysanthemum flower of spider form, together with leaves of *Iris japonica* arranged in a wide-mouthed vessel of compote type. Its main object of appreciation is the chrysanthemum flower, but the addition of leaves of *Iris japonica* has made the chrysanthemum look all the more beautiful. More than the contrasting beauty between soft orange and green, equilibrium of a certain hidden strength causes the chrysanthemum to look even more vivid. The techniques that were devised in those days when the *nageire* form had been brought into existence lay in making each of the two principal branches play the part of *in* (the negative) or *yoh* (the positive), and this form gradually developed into a new one, the *shoka* form, the third branch being added.

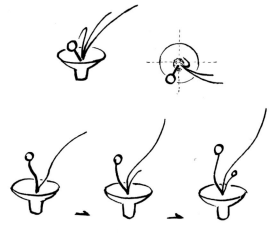

SHOKA

When we regard the *rikka* form as representing the elegant taste of nature, and the ordinary *nageire-moribana* form as representing the beauty of the plants shown in their parts, we can define the *shoka* form as representing the mood of a cluster of grass, or a plant as a whole. Of course, what *Ikebana* represents is not the apparent beauty of plants, but their figures that deal with the environment. Accordingly, it must be managed in such a way that we can perceive the environment of the plants just as they are in nature. When they are arranged as a work of *shoka,* therefore, we try to treat material plants in accordance with their supposed environment.

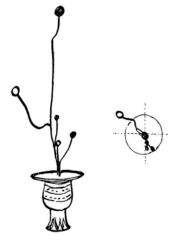

This photograph shows a work of juniper arranged together with small-flowered chrysanthemums in a copper vessel. It represents the figure of juniper tormented by wind and snow, yet which still endeavors to grow up, enduring these difficulties. In order to represent this mood in a single branch, the state of the branch of *soe* (assistant) branching out from the principal stem, and the position of the leaves, must have necessarily such posture exactly suitable to represent it, and again, with the aid of supplementary small flowers of chrysanthemum set in a youthful and vigorous shape, the work produces the deepest impression on spectators.

When you arrange water plants in a basin, it is important that the work should symbolize a spacious surface of water at its background with the water plants growing in groups. For this purpose, the basin should be amply filled with water, and the water plants are to be handled so as to represent the beauty to be extracted from the plant groups. Especially, when the plants are arranged in two groups, as this photograph shows, there should be represented such a state that the two will fuse into one, supplementing each other. This form is called *gyodo-ike*— "arranging along the course for fish"—where the work should be so composed that there exists an interval between the two groups not too long and not too short, and also that it displays a mood as if a fish swam about in a curved course.

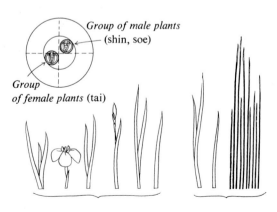

Female plants (Insertion order, from left to right)
Male plants (ditto)

This photograph shows a work of *tsuribana* (hanging down) style, its copper vessel symbolizing the moon; and here a beautiful sight of the moonlight seen through the branches has been introduced into an *Ikebana*.

This *shoka* is a work created by combining a branch of hydrangea, past the flowering season and with its leaves tinged with yellow, and Chinese bell-flowers, fresh purple in color, that are blooming as if to show a sign of autumn. The room is not ornamented by any picture or writing, and at the front of the alcove this *Ikebana* is hung so as to fill the room with fresh autumnal sentiment. A *tsuribana* arranged in a moon-shaped as well as a boat-shaped, vessel shows one of the *shoka* forms excellent in design and wit.

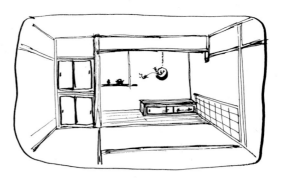

A bird's-eye view of composed branches. 95

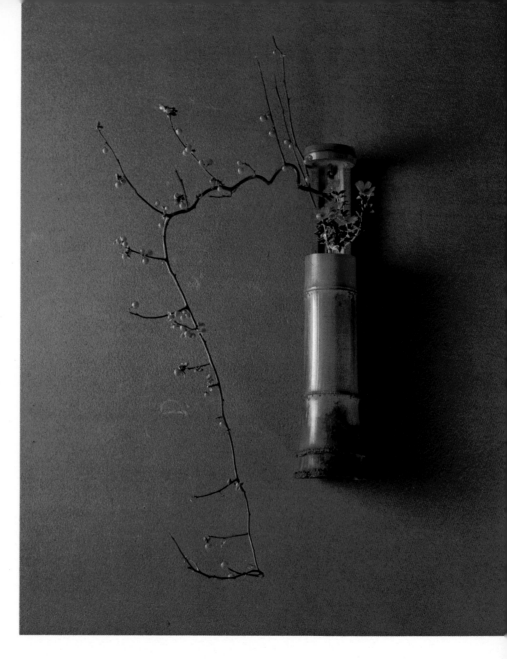

This photograph shows a work of bittersweet and small-flowered chrysanthemum arranged in a *ichijugiri-hanazutsu* (bamboo vessel with one opening). This style of *kakehana*, in which the vessel is hung to face the spectators, is called *mukigake* (hung facing the front), and that in which the vessel is hung to face sideways, *yoko-gake* (hung sideways). *Kakehana* style has a long-established tradition since the days of the old *nageirebana* form, and is suitable for those plants having a wind-blown nature or those having the habit of hanging down, into a proper shape, by following their natural condition. The disposition of the principal branch is to be determined mainly according to the nature of plants and their natural environment. The arranger aims at having the balance of *shin, soe,* and *tai* come out of itself, but he should set a higher value on the nature of the material than on the form of the work. He should keep in sight a mood in which the top-end of the branch tends to stretch upward in spite of its shape, which, according to its inherent nature, tends to hang down or to be bent by the wind.

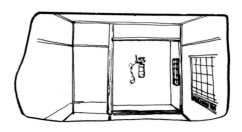

A large-flowered chrysanthemum displays serene emotion, being filled with simple and pure beauty. In order to make use of this nature when such plants are arranged, those that have stretched themselves freely are preferred to those that have crooked stems, so as to create an *Ikebana* of gentle appearance. The arranger should also treat the leaves and flowers equally with much care in arranging them into a shape of serene emotion, which displays noble beauty by representing proper and rigid control of the figure. This photograph shows a *shoka* of three chrysanthemums each having a large flower, arranged to-

gether with white-edged Eulalia grass. By adding pampas-grass, the stretching nature of the former becomes more effective, resulting in the increased effect here represented, which suggests to our mind its correlation to the environment where chrysanthemums grow.

As here, when leaves are added to the principal materials merely in order to supplement the figure of the latter and to increase the sentiment of a work, without maintaining independent figures in themselves, they are called *kariha*— borrowed leaves—one of the arranging techniques of *shoka*.

Preparation for *Shoka*

A suitable combination of flower vessel and materials is selected, and a *matagikubari* (wooden prop of Y-shape) is fixed into the vessel, which should be filled with enough water to reach the prop.

Methods of Arranging *Shoka*

First insert the branch nearest to hand in the crotch of the prop, then, pulling it closer by finger tip, add the second branch and the third, etc. until at last a *yokogi* (wooden chip to fill up to the gap) is added to firm up the whole.

Taking into consideration the strength and the nature of materials, the degree of the weight of the vessel, and the environment in which the *Ikebana* is decorated, the length of *shin* above the surface of the water is determined from one and a half to three times the height of the vessel. As for the *shin* branch, its *hiomote*—sunny front (surface that received the most light while it was growing)—should be put in a posture of stretching itself upward facing the sun imaginarily set in the rear right or leftward, and the whole figure should be in such a posture that the branch-top of *shin* can be seen in profile from the front side, while it assumes a posture of turning upon light, warping at a back corner and returning to

mid-air so as to rotate gradually that sunny front. The warping point of the waist should be a little lower than the middle of the *shin*, being laid out within the limit not to jut out of the vessel.

The *soe*, arranged behind the *shin*, is to direct its *hiomote* to the *shin*, drawing close to the latter, so as to assume such a posture as if it embraced the *shin*, stretching out toward the sun.

The length of its branch being two-thirds of the *shin*, the branch-top is to be laid out two times and a half of the warping depth of the *shin*.

The *tai*, arranged in front of the *shin*, being laid out to a front corner just in an opposite direction to *soe*, comes to show only the shade to the front side, its sunny front facing the sun. The length of

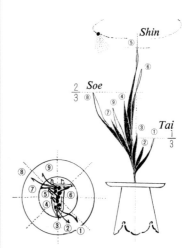

The insertion point and the way of assigning a position to each branch.

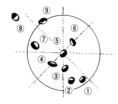

Distribution of branch-tops and the direction of hiomote *(the sunny front).*

this branch being 1/3 of the *shin*, the branch-top is to be laid out just in the same degree as the warping depth of the *shin*.

These photographs show a work of two large flowers of chrysanthemum of spider form, together with a small chrysanthemum, arranged in a copper vessel specifically named *shikainami* (gentle waves of the four seas), in which the *tai* is composed of three small-flowered chrysanthemums, while the *shin* and the *soe* are represented each by a large flower. In accordance with the degree of material strength, the *shin* and the *soe* are arranged each accompanied by the respective *ashirai* (supplementary branches), five, seven, nine...in total, that means odd numbers signifying a lucky omen. The photograph shows insertion order, beginning with the branches constituting the *tai* nearest to hand.

This photograph shows a *shoka* of five roses arranged in an arc-shaped vessel with a bright aspect, by which the arranger intended to display the enchanting beauty of the rose corolla. In arranging those flowers having a large corolla, especially as in chrysanthemum and rose flowers—those materials that have slightly, or rarely crooked stems, the effect will be quite different according to the way the flowers are distributed. In treating three corollas, usually each one is assigned to the *shin*, the *soe*, and the *tai* respecitvely; in the case of five, each two are assigned to the

shin and the *tai*, and *one* to the *soe;* in the case of seven, three are assigned to the *shin*, and each two to the *soe* and the *tai;* in the case of nine, it is usual to compose the work consisting of the three parts each with three corollas.

This *Ikebana* has been composed into a tringular form having an arc-shaped vessel as the base, and a corolla of *shin* as the apex, while the *soe* is laid out in large size, which gives variety to the positive stability of the entire figure, to the effect that it enlarges the space this work occupies.

In this *shoka* of blossoming loquats, the material, which does not appear beautiful so long as it remains as it is, has now become fit for producing an impressive work touching us to the heart, by expressing vivid rhythms of living plants.

It shows a composition different from the usual branch warping of fundamental *shoka* form; this is because the regular position of *yoh* (the positive of the sunny front) assumed on this *shoka* has been transferred to the right side via the back of this work, and each branch has undergone an organic change according to the transposition of *yoh* respectively. In this organic change, the actual state of living things has been displayed, and the beautiful balance is here suggested.

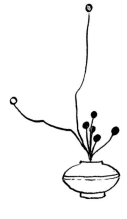

This is a work of *natsuhaze* (*Vaccinium ciliatum*) and chrysanthemums of medium-sized flowers, arranged in a copper vessel of a round bottle shape. In accordance with the nature of the vessel and materials, the arranger has enlarged the width of the structure so as to display the mildness of this work. Speaking of the nature of the material, those that grow on earth are stretching meekly, the sidelong extension should be reduced and the vessel also should be of a tall and strained cylindrical shape, but those that extend their branches sidewise, the wax-tree, for instance, should be arranged mildly into a sidelong extending figure, in a short yet wide vessel. Further, such materials that have a wind-bent or hanging-down property are to be arranged in a *kakehana* (hung flowers) or *tsuribana* (hung-down flowers) style, while water plants and the like are to be arranged in a basin representing the mood

of a water-side scene are to be formed into a specially variegated style. Now styles of *shoka* are classified into three main sorts, namely, the strained and rigid style, the slack or mild style, and the most freely designed style. The first is called *shin* (literally *truth* or "typical") style, the second is called *gyo* (literally *act* or "semi-typical") style, and the third is called *so* (literally grassy or "transformed") style.

This photograph shows a *shoka* of *gyo* style. The warping point of the *shin* branch has been set at a lower point, and in accordance with this warping, both the *tai* and the *soe* have been spread out with suitable warping. In the lights and shades of loquat leaves in autumnal tints, a mood of autumnal season can be amply felt, displaying the most beautiful contrast with the snow-white chrysanthemum.

Perceiving the vital energy of flowering plants deeply rooted in the maternal earth, by which they have built up their own shapes, leaving themselves to the hourly environmental changes and the atmospheric currents, an arranger tries to distribute properly the cut flowers and to arrange them in order to recreate them in a vessel—such is the Japanese *Ikebana.*

The combination of two materials—*kimmeichiku (Sinoarundinaria reticulata* var. *castillonus)* that appear to be swayed by the wind, submitting to the atmospheric current, and poet's narcissus that show pure and simple flowers'—displays their self-realizing force, while they assume free postures, yet without losing vigor to stretch themselves, nor descending to wanton figures. The gentleness caused by leaving themselves to the outside world combined with the tension overflowing in their interior allows a mood of elegant beauty to permeate the surroundings.

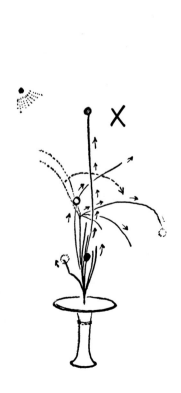

These photographs show a *shoka* of Japanese iris arranged in a wooden vessel symbolizing a small sailboat, that represents one of the traditional *shoka* forms. This figure symbolizes a boat lying at anchor and the flowers have been arranged in the *shin* style, because they constitute the subject that reminds us of the mast. Though I say this symbolizes an anchored boat, yet we must not forget the fundamental principles of arranging flowers. In this photograph, the flowers themselves represent the beauty of iris in the early spring. Preserving the pliability peculiar to the nature of iris, the beauty of these flowers, looking as if they bloomed just now, lies in the combination of leaves as well as in the height of open flowers and buds.

The beauty of *Ikebana* will be brought forth when natures of materials are kept alive so as to let certain flower-form follow after the former, the form being presumptively adopted.

This photograph shows a work of common broom together with azalea. The combination of azalea's habit of projecting branches in groups of a stair-like shape, with the posture of common broom in the blossom season that shows swaying at their branch tops while stretching up with springy impetus, has raised the consistent motion of a unified structure of different natures to the degree of beautiful rhythm. The movement of the azalea that juts forth from one side, moving gradually to the swaying common broom in zigzag motion, is the point worthy of note in this *shoka*.

When this technic is applied to a vessel of *nijugiri* (vessel with two insertion openings) by inserting each kind of plant separately into one opening, we get another style of *shoka* that is called *nijuike* (two-fold insertion), and following the way of treating azalea as seen in this photograph, when only the branches of this part are independently arranged in the lower opening, we get another style called *tachinobori-ike* (ascending style).

This photograph shows a *shoka* of *nijuike* in which flowers of *Thea sasanqua* are arranged in the upper insertion mouth, and staff-vine and iris in the lower opening. In *nijuike*, the two flower figures at the upper and the lower openings are, so to speak, to be fused onto one. *Nijuike* has two types, one is that in which flowers at the upper mouth are arranged in the larger figure, and those at the lower in the smaller figure, while the other type is just contrary to the former. The photograph shows a work which follows after the latter type. The larger parts have constituted the *shin* and the *soe* branches, while the smaller part has constituted the *tai*, both being fused into one. For this purpose, while the *shin*, the *soe*, and the *tai* are perceived in the respective parts, the arranger should confine the larger parts within the degree that permits us to perceive vaguely the *tai*, and make the smaller part display the action of the *tai*. These two parts, pulling and responding each other, show the beautiful current of lines and balance, while each of these two parts is working toward a different direction.

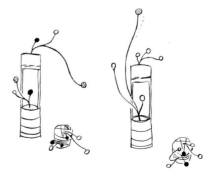

This photograph shows a *shoka* of *Spiraea cantoniensis* arranged in a hung-down vessel imitating a boat, that reminds us of a scene of a sailing boat that is running on the sea-surface with its swollen sail. The figure of flowers is constructed by the part of the sail and that of the scull. The part representing the sail shows the *shin* and the *soe* of the ordinary *shoka* form, and this part should necessarily be bent toward the bow so as to imitate a boat sailing before the wind, while the scull is to be laid out in large size toward the stern, and to this, at its lower part, is added a small branch corresponding to the *tai* in ordinary *shoka* form. Such a figure, in which the bow faces to the left, is considered to symbolize an outgoing boat, which means an *Ikebana* showing a very lucky omen.

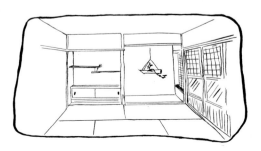

This is a *kakehana* of clematis arranged in a vessel of bamboo pipe equal in type to that shown on page 96. In order to make use of the material's nature, the arranger has adopted a composition that corresponds to the action of the branches. The vine here hanging down is assigned to the *shin*, the forceful winding part and the leaves attached to it are assigned to the *soe*, and one clematis flower is considered to constitute the *tai*. The ascending figure of vine-tips that wish to stretch up in the air indicates an earnest hope which the frail possess in common. As a *shoka* of *so*-style is to be composed according to the figure of the material being either hanging down or wind-bent, it is important not to overlook this earnest hope and incorporate it into the form of composition.

A plectrum-shaped board on which a flower-vase has been hung is called a *tarebachi* (hanging plectrum), contrived for the purpose of hanging a vessel on a wall where no nail is found.

A *shoka* is ordinarily composed of one or two sorts of plants, and this is because an arranger usually tries to make the beauty of plants most impressive, by abstracting the immutable principles lying in the intricate Mighty Nature and transferring them into this simple construction, but sometimes different sorts of materials, each keeping its own situation, are fused into one, to the effect that the whole produces a special mood, and for that purpose a technic called *sanshuike* (arranging three sorts) is adopted, where three sorts of materials are used. The assortment and composition of materials in *sanshuike* resemble that of *nishuike*.

This photograph shows a *sanshuike* of willow and plum branches and kale leaves, in which three sorts of materials, namely, willow branches that hang down gently, plum branches that extend fragrant and springy twigs, and kale leaves that show sidelong extension displaying beautiful coloring in spite of the severe cold, have produced pure and elegant atmosphere, without defying one another.

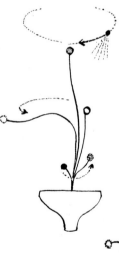

This photograph shows a *sanshuike* of Japanese iris, common pear blush (*Exochorda racemosa*), and fragrant plantain lily (*Hosta plantaginea*). In order to make the most of each material's property and to fuse them into one, the arranger adopted as his composing way both *gyakutai* (contrary-body type) and *soenagashi* (*soe*-flowing type), each of which is one of the highest techniques in the *shoka* form. The *gyakutai* is a type in which the direction of the *soe* and that of *tai* stretches out just contrary to the usual definite direction. The *soe-nagashi* is a type in which the *soe* is laid out far longer than is usual, while it is set in fluid motion, as if a liquid body flows out by itself. In order to compose a *shoka* of *sanshuike*, where to set assumptively the position of *yoh* will be·the key with which the arranger opens the door to either success or failure.

In this *shoka*, the arranger has transferred the *yoh*-point to a backward part of this work. As the result, the original *soe* leaving its traces in leaves of Japanese iris, the common pear blush that should take part of back accessory to the *shin* has been laid out in large size, expressing its function as the *soe*, and in accordance with this, a leaf of fragrant plantain lily has been given function operating toward the right. In co-operation of these three sorts of plants, brightness and impetus are well represented.

A work of *sanshuike* reproduced on page 109 has also been given similar composition to the former, but in this one *yoh* has been transposed to the rightward front, and the technique of *shinnagashi* (*shin*-flowing type)—letting the *shin* branch flow—has been jointly used.

A work of *sanshuike* reproduced here is composed of three materials, Japanese apricot, tulips, and Japanese iris, which make us feel positively the spring sunlight. The position of *yoh* has been set at the usual definite point of the rear of this *shoka*, only at a higher point near to mid-air. Accordingly, the Japanese apricot and the tulips also strongly represent such a force meekly stretching up, but the *Iris japonica* that should take part of the rear accessory of the *shin* has been extraordinarily swayed to the right in accordance with its own nature. Corresponding to the action of this *Iris japonica*, blades of tulip show a sign of movement to the left so as to keep a good balance. This work represents a mind deeply moved by the growing impetus of sprouting plants embraced in the arms of sunny spring.

A bird's-eye view of composed branches.

Rikka

Differing from the *shoka* form which makes us discover beauty of life in the appearance of a single plant, *rikka* leads us to represent a grand artistic effect revealed in a scenic beauty by arranging plants grown on a soaring peak or an extensively spreading field or a range of hills, each material cooperating with each other and unifying into one in spite of their various changes.

Most of the plants, though they stand in a complex situation, can be distributed in such a good balance between front and back, or right and left, that any material combination which might appear unnatural so long as it is seen separately comes to be given a due place respectively, so as to show an organic connection as an individual in the whole, which produces an impressive atmosphere by fusing into one harmonious body.

As for the fundamental principles, namely, that the arranged figure of flowers is composed with a balance of *in* and *yoh*, the proportion ratio of each part, and the way of treating materials, the *rikka* form does not differ from that of the *shoka*, but the *rikka* has the height of about 60 inches and the width of about 45 inches, and its arranged shape of flowers is massive, many pieces of materials being used, in such a way that it is composed of nine principal branches—*shin* (main branch), *soe* (assistant), *uke* (receiving), *nagashi* (flowing), *hikae* (accompanying), *mikoshi* (seen over, suggesting a vista), *shoshin* (real center), *doh* (trunk), and *maeoki* (anterior).

The *rikka* form has two styles, the one is called *sugushin* (direct *shin*), in which the "main" branch stretches up directly, and the other is called *nokijin* (once digressing *shin*), in which the top-end of the "main" branch, after once digressing to the right or left, returns to the center. The photograph shows a work of the first style with its "main" branch stretching up directly, which is fit to represent a tranquil and sublime emotion. A *rikka* of *nokijin* style includes various types, such as one in which the "main" branch digresses from the higher part of the central body, as is seen in the illustration below, and another in which the "main" branch digresses from the middle part, and then another in which its "main" branch digresses from the lower part, each of which corresponds both to the object of representation and to the nature of materials varied in its appearance, and all the principal branches other than the "main" branch also display the respective changes according to the change of the "main" branch.

Though the respective materials which constitute a *rikka* should reproduce their natural figures as truly as possible, it does not necessarily

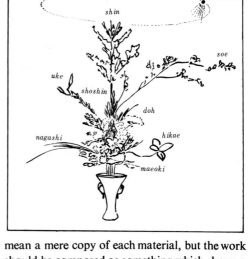

mean a mere copy of each material, but the work should be composed as something which shows a moment that reminds us of a certain scene behind itself, suggesting its environment that the work tries to depict. Various sorts of materials that have, in spite of their difference in color and figure, such figures and natures suitable for this supposed environment are selected. The substantial sympathy consisting in the various materials provides the bond that unifies the multifarious.

The photograph shows a *rikka* arranged on the basis of the key-note suggested by the scenic mood of the plants that adorn the foot of an autumnal mountain, representing the most impressive beauty of *natsuhaze (Vaccinium ciliatum)* tinted by the autumnal sunlight coming through a dense cluster of trees. For this purpose, the "assistant" branch of *natsuhaze* has been projected longer than usual, and the other branches also have been given a strained composition in response to the movement of the former, the whole displaying beautiful balance of strength.

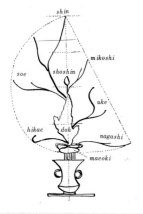

Graphical explanation of the fundamental construction of noki-jin-rikka.

Methods of Arranging *Rikka*

When a *rikka* is arranged, a deep vessel with a wide mouth is used. Accordingly a special device has been made. First, several straws are boundled into a stick, which is then bound with string at three points. Then several of these sticks are bound together again with string at three spots and inserted into the vessel.

As for the branches of flower material, those that have properly slanted figures in their present state are chipped aslant at the lower end, and each of those that do not have such figures is to be appropriately nailed up to another trunk with a sharpened end, then they are inserted into this bundle of straw. And as for flowering plants that have weak or short stems, an *ukezutsu*—a legged holding pipe—is prepared, which shall be first inserted, and then the plants are inserted into it.

When these preparations are completed, first the "main" branch is set up, and then the "receiving" branch which corresponds to the former, and the "assistant," the "flowering," the "accompanying," the "trunk,"...thus principal branches are to be inserted right and left alternately, good balance being taken into consideration.

Sometimes the arranger uses the natural shape of a branch as in the photograph, but in order to represent an ideal scenic mood, he usually adds some twigs and leaves in such a way that they may appear really natural. Among the principal branches, those of woody materials that take principal parts are to be inserted earlier, and to them twigs and leaves are added so as to adjust the figure, then, after the flowering plants that constitute the principal branches are inserted, accessory twigs or flowers are added.

The photograph shows a work which has been anomalously composed in such a way that the lower twigs of the "main" branch are covered as far as the upper part of the "receiving" branch, those twigs reserving their interesting taste, and in accordance with this irregular form, the "accompanying" branch has been laid out in large size, and the "receiving" and the "flowing" branches have been only vaguely activated by the flowering plants. This variation will be clearly comprehended when it is compared with a standardized form illustrated in the lower column.

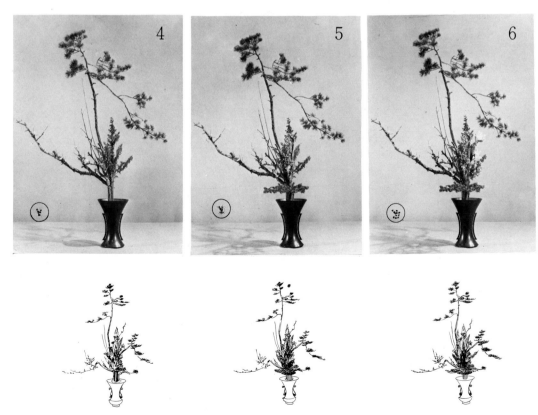

115

This photograph shows a *rikka* in which the arranger has made best use of simple material. Its figure has been simplified, the "vista" branch being omitted from the nine principal branches, with accessory branches also extremely diminished, to the effect that the function of principal branches has been all the more distinctly displayed, so that we can appreciate the simple beauty of this work.

Formally speaking, this is a work of *sugushin* style (direct *shin* style), yet the interesting shape of the pine branch, effectively applied as it is, has been laid out to the right in large size, and accordingly the "assistant" and the "accompa-

nying" branches have been made only slightly active, while the "receiving" and the "flowing" branches have been intensely activated in response to the "main" branch. Especially, as the "anterior" and the "flowing" branches also, pine branches have been used in order to set the focus of the structural interest on the function of these three principal branches. You can also find specific character in the way of handling narcissi that constitute the "accompanying" branch, handling the narcissus blades as if they were thrown out. Both of the two techniques, the "anterior" pine branch and the *nageha* (thrown blades) of narcissi, belong to the time-honored traditional styles of the *rikka* form.

The *rikka* form has a specific character in its complex composition as well as in the diversity of materials, and with respect to the following seven plants and trees, that is, pine, cherry-tree, iris, lotus, chrysanthemum, maple-tree, and daffodil, a special technique of *rikka* has been handed down to this day that the material should be limited to a single sort. It is a specific *rikka* form in which many beautiful phases of a single sort of material are arranged in order, so as to make them into one artistic work. We are deeply impressed by the variety of beauty consisting in a single sort of material.

This photograph shows a *rikka* arranged with iris only as a single kind of material, in which the beauty viewed in a group of iris blooming in purple and white can be clearly extracted.

By copying the natural figure, the flower constituting the "main" branch has been slanted toward *yoh* (leftward in this case), and in response to this movement, the "assistant" blade has been waved to a high degree. By the action of these two principal branches, postures of the "assistant" and the "flowing" branches activated in right-hand side can be automatically introduced. We perceive charming beauty of the young and fresh iris, overflowing of itself in its free and smooth posture.

This photograph of a *rikka* shows a grand view of a mountain-recess, its precipice being visible. The weather-beaten figure of an old pine tree with its lower branches is well expressed by the main, the assistant, the trunk, and the flowing branches; in the rightward side of *in*, a flowering plant has been secretly added, showing a strained feeling, and as the accompanying branch a brightly blooming rose was adopted.

Here the arranger has created a rigorous taste of elegant simplicity plus affability of those lying near-by.

An aged trunk stretching up with its treetop, swaying to the right, constitutes the main branch, and an old twig as the assistant branch has been activated as it is. Here a special style *hidari-nagashi* (leftward flowing style) has been applied, its flowing and accompanying branches coming forth just contrary to the ordinary way. In response to the rightward movement of the main branch, the flowing branch has been laid out to the left in large size, so as to make it well-balanced. This is a work of scenic representation; its technique is not a mere formal change of materials.

This photograph shows a *rikka* representing scenic beauty of an autumnal mountain. It has also such a figure, in the same way as the *rikka* illustrated on page 118, where the accompanying and the flowing branches have changed places with each other, but it differs from the former in that the main branch with weakened strength has been slanted to the right—that is, to the positive or sunny side, *yoh*—following its natural shape, and the receiving branch, which appears to be stronger than the main branch, has been strongly projected leftward, so that the flowing

and the accompanying branches have changed their places as was described, in order to keep a good balance by stretching the flowing branch far out to the right.

Five leaves of magnolia have been used as the trunk branch in this *rikka*. Broad leaves are often used at the inner part of the trunk branch in order to conceal the inserting spot of *ashirai* (accessory) branches, but here broad leaves were allotted for the part of the trunk branch itself, to the effect that the whole work expresses a freely stretching mood and ample sensations.

This photograph shows a *rikka* in which the arranger has tried to express his interest in the soft and gentle curves drawn by a drooping flowering cherry-tree that may be found in the bright sunbeams of the early spring.

The cherry branch constituting the main branch flows to the right in a large curved line. In the stretching manner of this branch lies the key point of success or failure of this *rikka*. With respect to a branch of this sort, as is already explained, it is important for the branch to possess such a soft movement, left to its surroundings like that of some liquid flowing out; in other words, it should not have a stout and stiff figure. The flowing branch, which is one of the principal branches, displays such a function, but in the present case, the interest of this function is alloted for the main branch. It is anomalous that the main branch is given such a function, and accordingly the plum yew of the assistant branch has been extended to the left in large size, while the accompanying branch is composed of a small pine branch, and the flowing branch composed of a tiny *baimo* (*Fritillaria thunbergii*) has been put in its place, less weight being attached to the same, and the accompanying branch has been treated in a more powerful figure than usual, so that the whole is able to keep a good balance. This is one of the types of *Ikebana* that require the most difficult techniques taught in the Ikenobo School.

This photograph shows a *rikka* which represents the throb of life as revealed in plants that are going to stretch their branches and make their flowers bloom in the coming spring. The main branch of *kobushi* (*Magnolia kobus*) and the flowing branch of pine tree, replete with strength in their appearance, express the swell of vital energy. The throb of life perceived in this *rikka* has been brought forth by the concord within the branches and their impetus.

The main branch, magnolia, flows toward the right, showing large curved lines, and the flowing pine branch which accepts the action of the former, after once flowing out leftward so as to keep the balance of right and left, shows a sign of turning back to follow after the action of the former. Chrysanthemums employed as the accompanying branch show a sign of revolving movement from the right to the upper left side, as if it tried to stop the former movement, and the second movement turning round into the stream of the leaves of Japanese iris which constitute the vista branch, flows out rightward in a large curved line. In the movement of camellia branches and leaves also, which tightens the strained effect of the lower part, a sign corresponding to it can be perceived. We can also find the balance of strength in those which correspond and pull one another, and the movement of branches changing from strained form into fluid phase. These moments have been unified into one in representing a work filled with the vivid appearance of life.

The photograph below shows an *Ikebana* arranged by following the composing techniques in a smaller scale, diminishing the number of branches as far as possible, in order to introduce a modern sense into this work. For the movement of the branches and the manner of their corresponding to one another, the fundamental principle of *rikka* is adopted as it is, yet in order to set up each branch, a *kenzan* (a needle-point holder) is used, treated in the same way as in the *nageiremoribana* (thrown-in and piled-up) form. As for the flower materials, *Strelitzia reginae*, acacia, and the like are used, which express bright and neat sense, so as to develop a *rikka* form which fits into modern living.

Looking back to its historical passage, the present *Ikebana* of the Ikenobo School is proceeding on its way, attempting incessantly to develop a new phase. Having its long history, *Ikebana* should always co-exist with our own livelihood, as a living thing of the present age in itself.

The very common feeling of human life felt in the attitude of those who look at flowering plants is the fundamental origin from which *Ikebana* comes into existence.

Seeking for "reliance upon the future" in *Ikebana*, a man, in daily life, arranges flowers, appreciates flowers, always entertaining his expectation toward the peaceful and fruitful world.

THE OHARA SCHOOL

By Houn Ohara

*Translated by Ruth Dillon
and Fukiko Yamaguchi*

Unshin Ohara, founder and first headmaster of the Ohara School and originator of the now extremely popular *moribana* style, served his apprenticeship as a ceramic artist in a family famous for its ceramic art. He studied *Ikebana* of the Ikenobo School under his father from the time of his early youth, as an avocation, but eventually began to take this avocation more and more seriously. The turn of the century brought many changes to Japan, including the importation into Japan of the lavishly colored flowers of the Western world. With his imagination stimulated by the vivid colors of the imported flowers, Unshin Ohara began to include them in his arrangements of *Ikebana*. Finding the formal, upright style of Ikenobo completely unsuitable for these new plants, he developed a wholly new style that used low, wide containers. These flat, shallow containers permitted a more casual arrangement that soon progressed to the "natural scenery" *moribana* that were to change the whole future of *Ikebana*.

Moribana means, literally, "piled-up flowers in a flat basin," and represented the first serious attempt to utilize Western flowers in Japanese flower arrangements. Like most innovations in a highly conservative culture, the appearance of *moribana* drew much criticism and even received complete rejection by the masters of the traditional styles. The Japanese people, however, welcomed this fresh and colorful style, found that it could be learned with comparative ease, and immediately adopted it. Early in the present century, Unshin Ohara broke away from the Ikenobo School and staged a public exhibition of *moribana*-style arrangements to celebrate the founding of the Ohara School. The Ohara School was an instant success both in Japan and abroad, and has attracted literally millions of students; Houn Ohara is the third-generation headmaster. The photographs that accompany this chapter well illustrate the charm and beauty of the *moribana* style. However, it should be emphasized that the *moribana* style of the Ohara School still possesses many bonds with the traditional styles of *Ikebana* from which it sprang. Through *moribana*, skilled flower arrangers, who have experienced the joy of interpreting the spirit of nature in their own handiwork, are inspired to communicate to their fellowmen the expression of their recognition and appreciation of nature's beauty, which, after all, is the basis of *Ikebana* as an art.

W.C.S.

Ikebana in the Ohara School

THE BASIC FORMS

Basically, *Ikebana* of the Ohara school is classified into two primary categories: *moribana* and *heika*—or *nageire*, as it is commonly called.

Moribana arrangements are those made in a low bowl. This may be a small compote, a flat plate, a wide shallow basin, or any similar shape in which water may be contained if needed. Usually a holder—either a needle-point holder (*kenzan*) or a heavy metal holder with separated openings (*shippo*)—is employed.

Heika or *nageire* arrangements are those made in a tall container, a bottle-shaped or cylindrical vase, or any vessel having depth. Usually such containers have a smaller opening than the low bowl, and ordinarily no holder of any kind is employed in the placement of materials.

A careful study of materials, to learn to determine the basic form—*moribana* or *heika*—most suitable for their arrangement, and to select an appropriate container, is a most important step to good harmony in arrangements, for the container does much more than merely contain the flowers; it becomes an essential part of the total design.

THE FIVE BASIC STYLES

The two basic *Ikebana* forms may be interpreted in the lines of five different Ohara styles—the style being the shape outlined by the principal materials. Three main branches—subject, secondary and object—form the foundation or framework in each style. The length and position of these three stems differ in each style, the result being in each case three main points forming a triangle of different shape and dimensions. The proportionate lengths of the principal stems are predetermined to assure a well-balanced structure; however, the container itself is the controlling factor in determining actual measurements and angle of inclination of stems. The position of the arrangement, considered from the viewer's angle, is also an important influence. The first step is always to consider the material itself.

As you will see, each style is designed to bring out a particular aspect of the beauty of materials, by emphasizing their highly individual characteristics. Good judgement in the choice of style must coincide with the proper selection of form and container in order to achieve a successful arrangement. Study and practice, plus experience gained through handling a wide variety of materials, are the requisites for acquiring this kind of judgement.

To complete the design begun with the container and three main branches or stems, additional materials, known as fillers, become a part of the arrangement. Fundamentally, they fill in the outline provided by the main stems. Their purpose may be to accent, to contrast, to provide movement, to emphasize a mood or atmosphere, or to supply the unexpected touch that lifts an arrangement from the ordinary to the artistic, while always playing a supporting role to the principal stems.

Both *moribana* and *heika* forms are classified into five styles:

> Upright style
> Slanting style
> Cascade style
> Heavenly style
> Contrasting style

In both forms, and in all five styles, we find variations and free styles.

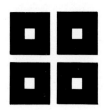

An example of natural method.

THE FIVE METHODS

The next step, after determining the appropriate style for the material, is to decide upon the method. What is the point to be emphasized? Color? Line? Volume? The various methods are designed to bring out and enhance the characteristics that will produce the desired effect. An atmosphere of feeling may also be expressed by controlling the method of arrangement, as you will learn. The five methods include:

> Natural method
> Color-scheme method
> Mass-effect method
> Line-scheme method
> Abstract method

These five methods in turn fall into one of two classifications: natural and color-scheme methods follow the realistic trend; mass-effect, line-scheme, and abstract arrangements are classified as non-realistic. These trends are explained in more detail later on.

Natural

To express this in a fuller sense we might say a "method of presenting nature as it is," this being a translation of the Japanese term for this method. This is believed to have been the fundamental idea behind all *Ikebana*—to present plant-life as it is seen from season to season, to express a love of nature by reproducing, imaginatively, a portion of her beauty within the small sphere of a flower container. It is the essence of this beauty, with nonessentials removed, that is translated by the *Ikebana* artist. To recognize the beauty in every aspect of nature requires daily observation, for it is not to recreate an arrested moment of beauty that we wish, but to imbue the arrangement with the life and movement that exist in nature, without which it will be static and meaningless.

Color-scheme

The purpose of this method is to emphasize the beauty of color in materials, by combining colors which harmonize, contrast, or complement each other. To achieve this purpose, the natural growing characteristics and seasonal significance of material are sometimes disregarded; however, good design is never sacrificed for color effect. Balanced composition is essential. More effective distribution of color is possible by skillful composition of a design, using the varied lengths and positions of materials to bring out or subdue a color, to point up a contrrast or to blend harmoniously. The colors themselves may be selected to create a soft, quiet beauty, or a joyous gaiety.

Colors are extremely important in all Japanese flower arrangement, having profound psychological influence upon human beings, as well as reflecting the cultural tastes and personality of the arranger.

Mass-effect

Modern *Ikebana* has developed through the need for stronger expression, in keeping with the urgency and stress encountered in daily life. Creative urges have been stimulated by postwar trends and developments found in all phases of our existence.

The mass effect enables the arranger to meet this need for stronger design by utilizing volume to produce emphasis. Massed chrysanthemums, for example, are much more striking in color as part of a design than individual flowers would be.

Massing is usually done by grouping and tying materials before arranging, rather than attempting to arrange individual stems for the desired appearance.

Line-scheme

The opposite of the mass-effect method, but equally important, the line-effect arrangement uses every line of the material in the production of the desired design. Not only the line, but the space around it, becomes a part of the arrangement, and it is possible to express strong movement artistically by skillfully arranging lines in rhythmic patterns. *Ikebana* has developed along with Japanese painting, and a strong mutu-

An example of color-scheme arrangement.

al influence is inherent in the two arts; however, the line-effect has developed even more rapidly in modern *Ikebana*. Geometric detail and directional emphasis in line arrangement are the result of the application to *Ikebana* of techniques used in modern abstract painting.

Abstract

The use of materials other than plant-life in *Ikebana* is usually attributed to the newer, modern trends; however, in *rikka*, the oldest known form of *Ikebana*, sand and stones were used in some arrangements. This indicates that there has long been recognition of the unexpected beauty to be found in objects and materials other than flowers. To find this beauty and to enhance it by adapting the material to a design, either alone or in combination with similar materials, or with living plants, requires a keen eye and artistic sense.

As a ceramic artist begins with clay to form a thing of beauty, so the *Ikebana* artist assembles iron, plaster, stones, glass, etc. to express his recognition of the kind of beauty to be found therein by composing an artistic design.

THE TRENDS

In the early days of the Ohara School, when *Ikebana* was only a means of artistically expressing appreciation of the beauty of nature, the natural and color-scheme methods of arrangement alone existed and were practiced in both *moribana* and *heika* forms; the natural to interpret the beauty of scenery, the color-scheme to emphasize to the fullest the beauty of colorful materials.

Recognition of the individual beauty to be found in colors and shapes of plants and flowers brought about a new trend, using each material as part of a design, rather than as its natural self.

Realistic arrangement

Whether combined in a natural scenery arrangement, or as individual plants, materials arranged realistically are displayed exactly as they appear in life, their beauty enhanced by the idealistic and imaginative touch of the arranger.

Non-realistic arrangement

In non-realistic arrangements, each material becomes an object—a shape, a color, a line—completely without regard for the manner in which it grew. The combination of materials into an arrangement becomes the creation of a design. Flowers, branches, leaves and roots may be composed in a pattern altogether contrary to their natural aspect. Startlingly different from the arrangements of the old days, which were imitations of nature, these non-realistic designs bring out a greater depth of loveliness, through stronger emphasis on the forms of materials. For example, the mass-effect arrangement is a more emphasized form of color-scheme, and belongs to the non-realistic, because it does not conform to the natural growth of the materials.

An example of non-realistic arrangement.

Basic Rules for *Moribana*

The numerous kinds of arrangements in the Ohara School begin from basic fundamentals. The most basic *moribana* arrangement is made in a shallow round container, usually having a diameter of 12 to 15 inches.

Just as a rough sketch is made in preparation for a painting, a rough outline must be planned for an arrangement. Follow this explanation on the accompanying diagrams:

Within the circle representing the container a square is outlined with corners designated A B C D. A line drawn from A to D forms an isosceles triangle of ABD (diagram 2-A). Within this triangle the arrangement is to be made. A and B being on a straight line, however, would result in some material concealing that directly behind it, and would spoil the final effect. By dividing the line into fifths (diagram 2-B) and moving B point one-fifth of the distance towards A point (diagram 2-C) we move B from directly in front of A and at the same time change the shape of the triangle slightly. When only a few materials are to be used, the size of the triangle may be reduced by moving point D nearer to B (diagram 3).

The point of this triangle from which the arrangement will be started is determined by (1) the characteristics of the material, (2) the size and shape of the container, and (3) the location and position from which the arrangement will be viewed. These three points determine the style and the direction of the arrangement, and placement of the holder (*kenzan* or *shippo*).

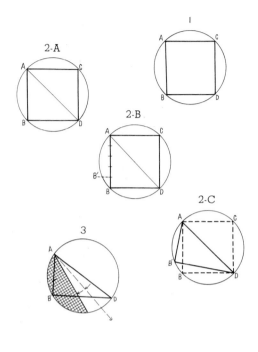

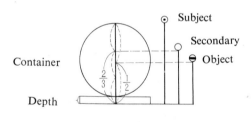

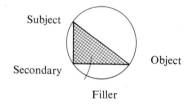

Basic directions
for the *moribana* upright style

The three principal stems, arranged first, are placed with the subject at point A, the secondary at B and the object at D.

The proportion of these three stems remain substantially the same, the secondary being two-thirds the length of the subject and the object one-half the length of the subject. The measurement of the subject is determined by the size of the container, and for the sake of good balance may vary from the basic measurement as shown in diagram 4—the diameter plus the depth of the container—to a length measuring twice the diameter of the

container or more. Characteristics of the materials used and the nature of the container influence this measurement. By experimenting, it is possible to achieve the ideal length for the conditions mentioned.

Within the triangle—called the intermediate space—formed by the three principal stems, the fillers are added; their purpose, as stated earlier, is to support and enhance the three main stems and to round out the composition.

Basic Rules for *Heika*

Heika and *nageire* are synonymous terms for an arrangement done in a tall vase—even a single flower in a bud vase. Even in containers having a very small opening, the space to be devoted to the arrangement is an important consideration. Regardless of the size of the container, only one-fourth of the opening is to be utilized in the placement of materials (diagram 1). The arrangement may be done in either the left front quarter or the right front quarter of the vase opening. No holder is used. Stems are secured by the methods shown on page 146, diagram C.

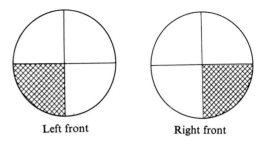

Left front   Right front

Basic directions for the *heika* slanting style

In the slanting style, the three principal stems will be positioned as shown in diagram 2. The subject inclines forward at a 50-degree angle and 45 degrees to the left of center front. The secondary converges with a line drawn back from the point where the subject touches the edge of the container. The object is placed at a 30-degree angle to the right of center front (diagram 2).

As in the basic measurements for *moribana*, the length of the subject is determined by the size of the container, the basic measurement being one-half to two times the height of the container. Varying according to the kind of material used, the subject may be more than twice the height of the container and remain in good balance. The secondary may be one-half to two-thirds the length of the subject, and the object, about one-half of the subject. These measurements include only the visible portion of the material, and the length of stem resting inside the container must be in addition to the prescribed lengths. Fillers are used as in *moribana* to support the principal stems and complete the composition. No strict rules govern their length and distribution.

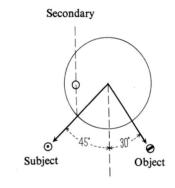

Secondary

Subject 45° 30° Object

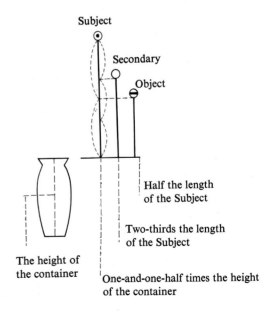

Subject

Secondary

Object

Half the length of the Subject

Two-thirds the length of the Subject

The height of the container

One-and-one-half times the height of the container

UPRIGHT STYLE—*MORIBANA*

This is the most common of the basic styles, being a composition of serene simplicity. Its significance lies in the subject, which is arranged in an upright position at the left rear of the container. The secondary is placed at a 45-degree slant, 30 degrees to the left front, while the object is placed at a 60-degree forward slant, and about 45 degrees to the right. These three stems form the principal line of the basic upright style.

The arrangement may be composed in exactly the reverse position, to accomodate materials or location of the arrangement to better advantage, by beginning from a subject arranged at the right rear. Added materials to complete the arrangement are known as fillers. Two *shippo* are used, placed as illustrated. One large *kenzan* may be substituted.

Upright Style—*Moribana*

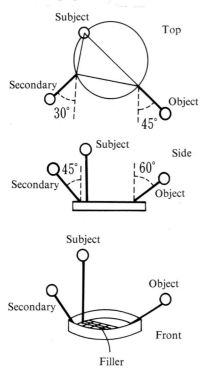

Diagram and pictures illustrate the basic moribana *upright style, using two varieties of chrysanthemums.*

(A) The subject, its length totaling one and one-half times the diameter of the container, and the secondary, measuring two-thirds the length of the subject, are placed as shown in the diagram and explained above.

B

C

D

(B) A filler, one-half the length of the subject, is added between the subject and secondary, in the same holder with the subject.

(C) Four smaller double-headed chrysanthemums, as fillers, are arranged. One, to the right of the subject, is placed in the rear holder with the flower appearing between subject and large filler. All others are placed in the front holder: one slanted forward on the right; another cut short and placed at the foot of the secondary; and a third slanted forward, very low, between the first two.

(D) Finally, the object—another double-headed chrysanthemum—one-half of the subject in length, is placed as shown in the diagram, facing towards the right front, to complete a basic style *moribana* arrangement of three large chrysanthemums and five small double ones.

UPRIGHT STYLE—*HEIKA*

In the basic upright style for a tall vase arrangement, the principal consideration is to achieve a tall, slender appearance, rather than a widespread one, so it is essential to arrange materials compactly at the point where they emerge from the vase. The subject is arranged at the left front, slanted twenty degrees forward. The secondary, at a 70-degree forward slant, points 30 degrees to the left front from the base of the subject, appearing to be from the same stem. The object is placed at an 80-degree forward slant, facing almost directly forward. Fillers are added to complete the basic line formed by these three principal stems.

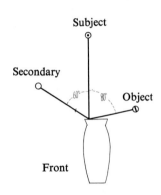

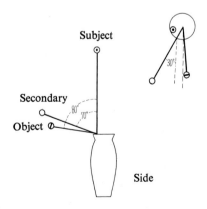

Diagram and pictures illustrate the basic heika *upright style, using Japanese magnolia tree and roses in a black vase.*

Using the methods illustrated on page 146 for securing stems in container:

(A) The subject—two and one-half times the height of the container—is placed at the left front corner, slanted slightly forward. The small attached branch is natural, and does not interfere with the line.

(B) The secondary—one-half the length of the subject—emerges from the vase on the right of the subject and crosses to the left. It is actually a horizontal side branch, the upper part of the main branch having been trimmed off, the lower part forming the base of the secondary stem. This procedure should be followed in using materials which are brittle or not easily curved. One flller-branch is added at the left of the subject, and another below the secondary, slanted low and forward.

(C) Because Japanese magnolia branches have buds only at the tips, leafy material should be selected to combine with them. Lily, camellia, mustard-flower, or—as used here—roses, may be suitably combined with the Japanese magnolia. One tall rose is arranged at the back of the subject, tilted forward. A second rose is used as the object, placed directly at the front of the arrangement as shown in the diagram. Finally, a third rose, about one-half the length of the first one, is added between the two. Leaves are carefully adjusted to fill the area just above the container without appearing cluttered or crowded.

SLANTING STYLE—*MORIBANA*

In this style the position of the subject and secondary are the reverse of the upright style; however, the position of the holder remains unchanged. The subject inclines forward, the secondary is placed at the rear. The emphasis is thus placed on the beautiful forward slanting line of the principal material, making this an appropriate style for tree branches and plants with a naturally slanting line.

The subject is placed at the left front corner of the container, extending 45 degrees to the left, slanted forward 70 degrees. The secondary is placed at the back of the subject, slanted just slightly to the left. The position of the object is the same as in the upright style, placed at the center front, 50 degrees forward slant and at about a 30-degree angle to the right. These three stems form a scalene triangle, with the point of the subject reaching well beyond the edge of the

container. Basic measurements are frequently disregarded in the slanting style, and individual characteristics of materials are considered to determine the most attractive proportions. Often it becomes necessary to shorten the customary length of the secondary—two-thirds that of the subject—to about one-half the length, to avoid an unbalanced look.

Lilies retain their fresh appearance longer than most cut flowers. With their pure whiteness and strong leafy stems, they are ideal for this *moribana* color-scheme arrangement. Basic measurements for the *moribana* arrangement being shorter than those for *heika*, fuller, leafier stems are more suitable; however, too many stems or flowers may result in cluttered disharmony when combined with other materials. Consideration should be given to buds which may open after the arrangement is finished.

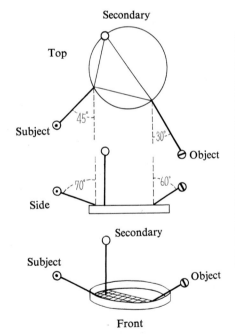

Illustrated is a basic moribana *slanting style, combining white trumpet lily, double camellia and small-flowered chrysanthemums in a twice-baked shallow bowl.*

(A) A strong-looking double-budded lily is selected as the subject, cut to measure one and one-half times the diameter of the container, and arranged at the left front as previously explained. Buds should be poised carefully to avoid a drooping appearance. The secondary—one-half of the subject—is then placed at the back of the subject, slanted slightly to the left. The space between these two principal stems is minimized by the strong inclination of one bud towards the subject.

(B) One lily—a tall filler—is placed at the base of the secondary, its tip tilted towards the object. Careful attention must be given to the angles of both buds and stems in placing these three most important flowers, for a unified composition.

(C) The large camellia blossoms are cut short and placed low, to avoid distracting from the subject. A minimum of trimming provides a leafy frame, so the flowers are softened rather than highlighted. One full blossom is placed beside the tall filler, slanted slightly forward. The second, with a leafy budded branch attached, slants very

low from the right of the subject. Trimming—only enough to remove crowded leaves—is done after stems are in place.

(D) Three stems of clustered small white chrysanthemums are used as object and companion fillers. Superfluous buds and flowers are trimmed and stems are cut for mass. The object is placed first, low at the right front, with one filler between it and the camellia and the second filler behind these two to provide depth.

Three roses and pine may be combined with lilies for a similar arrangement.

SLANTING STYLE—*HEIKA*

This is perhaps the most ideal style for displaying the lovely natural lines of plant materials as they grow.

Spring and early summer bring the fresh green verdure so refreshing and eye-catching in natural arrangements. Maple is one of the most beautiful of the spring foliage.

(A) Using the method diagrammed on page 146 for securing stems in the container, the subject more than twice the height of the container, is placed slanted 50 degrees forward and 45 degrees to the left (pointed in the direction of the left shoulder) with the secondary, one-half the length of the subject, drawn back of the subject, slightly to the left. Only the most crowded leafiness should be trimmed, using care not to destroy the natural look.

(B) A short branch of young leaves is placed close to the base of the subject, slanted forward, curving over the edge of the container. Back of the subject, another branch is placed to develop the natural, leafy appearance. Basic rules call for an odd number of branches; however, because of the leafy character of the materials, a long attached twig on the secondary may be regarded as the fifth stem, rather than crowd the container with the addition of a separate branch.

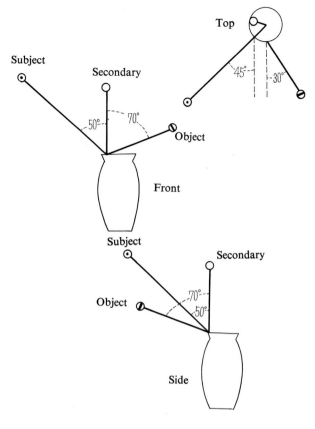

Illustrated is a basic heika *slanting style, using full moon maple and Spiraea cantoniensis.*

A

B

(C) Disregarding the usual combining materials such as chrysanthemum, lily, or other flowers, this arrangement features two woody-materials, which complement each other for added natural loveliness. One tall stem of spiraea forms an important filler, two shorter ones fill in the lines of the composition.

(D) Finally the object, one-third the length of the subject, is placed slanted 50 degrees forward and slightly to the right from the base of the subject. A last blossoming stem of spiraea is placed close at the top of the container. The most important point to remember in achieving a successful arrangement is to keep all stems as compactly arranged as possible where they emerge from the top of the container.

CASCADE STYLE—*MORIBANA*

As the designation suggests, this style is ideal for vines, for materials which twine or suspend, or materials having great natural flexibility. (Wisteria, akebia and bittersweet are examples.)

Its individuality and significance lie in the emphasis on line and movement, and to bring out these characteristics of materials to best advantage only a few materials are arranged together.

The basic regulations for the placement of materials are the same as for the slanting style;

however, because the subject curves downward, usually reaching below the base of the container, a high shelf or table is the most suitable location for an arrangement in the cascade style. With the subject resting at an angle of about 120 degrees and 45 degrees to left of center front, the secondary, placed behind it, is almost upright, drawn slightly backward to provide balance. The object has a forward slant of about 45 degrees, and a 30-degree angle to the right.

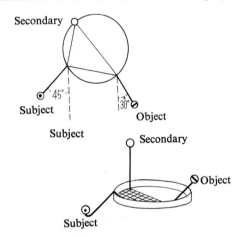

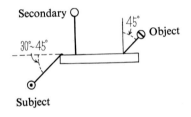

Diagram and pictures illustrate the basic moribana cascade style, using fasciated willow and double headed chrysanthemum in a round celadon-green container.

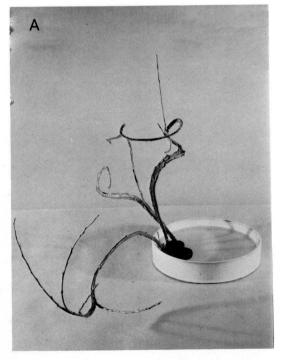

(A) The forward-inclining curve of the subject being the most important line in the cascade style, it is arranged with considered care. Its natural curves may be increased by bending, and the effect should be graceful, never drooping. The subject is placed at the left front corner of the holder, and the secondary, one-half the length of the subject, is placed behind it, slanted slightly to the left rear. A tall filler, almost the same length as the subject, is placed at the right of the subject, slanted forward to a lesser degree, and slightly to the right.

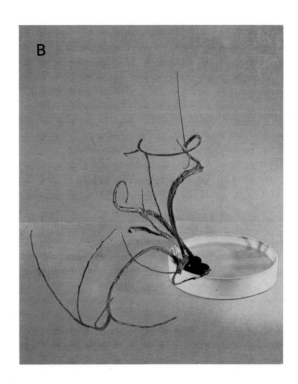

(B) Two short fillers—about half the length of the secondary—are added: one between subject and secondary, slanted forward and to the left, and a second to the right of the subject, curved forward over the edge of the container.

(C) The object, a chrysanthemum about half the length of the subject, is placed at the right front. Two short chrysanthemums are used as fillers, the first between the subject and short front filler of willow, and a second, even shorter, behind the first. The lines of the willow are cleanly revealed above the flowers, which are much shorter than usual in this particular combination.

CASCADE STYLE—*HEIKA*

In the *heika* form of cascade style, measurements may vary according to the materials selected. Frequently, vines are permitted to cascade to a length three or four times the height of the container, to display their natural beauty of line to greater advantage.

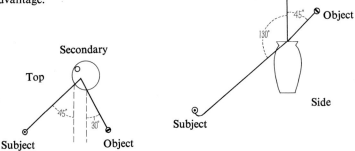

Diagram and pictures illustrate the basic heika *cascade style, using bittersweet, chrysanthemum and the tassels of maize in a tall ceramic vase of celadon-green.*

(A) The charming branch of bittersweet forms the subject, and is suspended from the left front corner of the vase, permitted to fall in a natural curve, so that the line is clearly distinguished and uncluttered. (see page 146)

The secondary, one-half the length of the subject, has a lifted line, and is drawn towards the back of the container, to give depth to the arrangement, and to balance the forward weight of the subject. A fuller branch is suitable for this particular stem.

(B) Three fillers of bittersweet are added. Note that they follow, to some extent, the existing lines formed by subject, secondary and container. The first filler curves forward over the container, just to the right of the subject. The second is behind the subject, tilted upward between it and the secondary, and the third slants very close to the subject, supporting and emphasizing the cascading main line.

(C) Three double-headed chrysanthemums are added as the object and fillers. One filler appears behind the subject, tall and almost erect, and a shorter one in front of the subject. The object slants strongly forward and slightly to the right. Chrysanthemum leaves have been trimmed in order not to clutter the slender lines of the bitter-sweet. Larger chrysanthemums would have an undesirably heavy appearance in comparison to the delicate line.

(D) The two tassels of maize placed in a natural attitude among the other materials provide an interesting autumnal accent.

HEAVENLY STYLE—*MORIBANA*

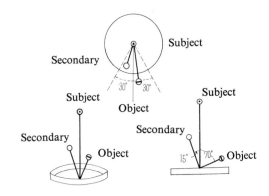

In this style the significance lies in enhancing the vertical line of the material. The subject is arranged at the center of the container. Basic measurements shown for materials are minimum lengths, and frequently materials are used considerably longer in order to display characteristics to advantage. The secondary is placed either to the right or left of the subject with a 15-degree forward slant.

All materials are confined within a space of 30 degrees to the right or left, with the subject at the top of the triangle and with a very compactly arranged base. Secondary and filler branches are shorter in proportion to the subject than in other styles, to further emphasize the vertical line. The object is placed very low—salnted forward about 70 degrees—at the front of the arrangement.

Diagram and pictures illustrate the basic moribana *heavenly style, using Dutch iris, chrysanthemums, and fern fronds in a rectangular compote.*

(A) The subject—more than twice the diameter of the container in length—is arranged upright at the center of the container. The secondary—one-half the length of the subject—is placed to the right front of the subject slanted forward as explained above. A shorter filler appears behind the subject, to the left.

(B) Ferns as fillers and Dutch iris as the object are placed close at the base of the subject, slanted forward but not spread wide at the sides. The object is one-third the height of the subject.

HEAVENLY STYLE—*HEIKA*

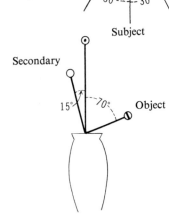

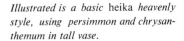

This style emphasizes vertical lines, requiring materials which grow naturally tall and straight. As in the *moribana* heavenly style, the subject is arranged at the center of the container, slanted forward about 10 degrees. The secondary may be placed at either the right or left of the subject, with a 30 degree forward slant. The object, placed directly in front of the subject, has a 70-degree forward slant. All stems should emerge from the container at one point, as compactly as possible.

Illustrated is a basic heika *heavenly style, using persimmon and chrysanthemum in tall vase.*

(A) The subject—more than twice the height of the container—(secured in place by one of the methods diagrammed on page 146) is placed in the center as explained earlier, with the secondary—one-half the length of subject—placed to the right. Placed behind the subject, a filler branch in good balance with the secondary.

(B) Two double-headed chrysanthemums are added as fillers: one between the subject and secondary and the other very short at the base of the secondary.

(C) The object—one double-headed chrysanthemum—is then inserted very low, slanted 70 degrees directly forward as shown in the diagram.

CONTRASTING STYLE—*MORIBANA*

Just as there are materials whose beauty is best displayed by standing them erect, and those which appear more graceful when slanted, there are materials whose characteristics are best displayed in a symmetrically balanced arrangement, and for these materials, the contrasting style is the most desirable composition, having as its keynote the beauty symmetry.

The subject is placed in the center of the container, extending to the side within a 30-degree area forward or to the back. The angle of inclination of the subject is not restricted, being determined by the individual characteristics of the material being used. The secondary crosses the subject closely at its base and extends in the opposite direction, at an inclination to provide at the same time balance and variety with the subject. The object is placed in the center with a forward slant of 70 degrees. Variety in length of materials provides symmetrical balance without being monotonous or static.

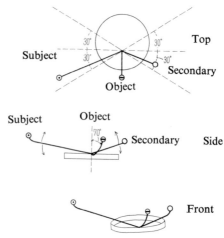

Pictures and diagrams illustrate the basic moribana *contrasting style, using bald acacia and calla lily in a Turkish blue compote.*

(A) The subject—more than twice the diameter of the container in length—extends to the left and about 15 degrees forward. The secondary—about one-half of the subject in length—crosses at the base of the subject stem to extend to the right at a slightly more horizontal level than the subject, and slightly toward the front of the container.

(B) Three additional fillers of the same material are arranged: one about one-third of the subject, placed between subject and secondary, slightly slanted to the rear: a second, shorter one conforming to the line of the secondary, just above it, and a third, short filler at the base of the arrangement, slanted forward over the edge of the container.

(C) The object—one-third the length of the subject—is placed at the center front, as shown in the diagram and explained above. Two calla lilies are added as fillers, above and behind the object, blended with the bald acacia fillers. A lovely symmetry is achieved, not strict enough to destroy the appeal of this contrasting style, but well balanced and in good harmony.

CONTRASTING STYLE—*HEIKA*

While recognizing the symmetrical beauty in materials for which the contrasting style is appropriate, it is also important to learn to recognize those for which the *heika* style is more suitable than the *moribana*.

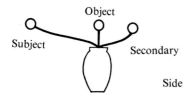

Diagram and pictures illustrate the basic heika contrasting style, using forsythia and snapdragon in a tall black vase.

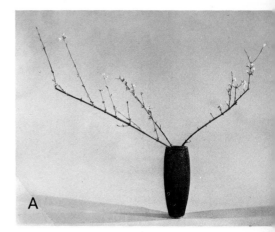

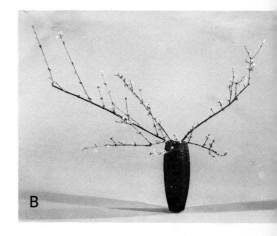

(A) The subject—more than twice the height of the vase in length—and the secondary—one-half the length of the subject—are arranged as shown, crossing at the base and extending in opposite directions in the front half of the vase opening. Firmly fixed main branches provide a good foundation for placing flowers correctly. (see page 146)

Both should slant a little forward; however, they should not touch the rim of the vase.

A short filler is inserted at the foot of the subject, its tip extending behind the subject, at a slightly more erect angle.

(B) Two smaller fillers are added in front, similar in proportions to the subject and secondary. Their tips extend below the base opening in front, to provide a tie between materials and container.

(C) Three snapdragons are placed within the frame provided by the forsythia. The object flower slants strongly forward, the fillers being more upright, the three stems arranged close together in the vase.

Use of the *Kenzan* and *Shippo*

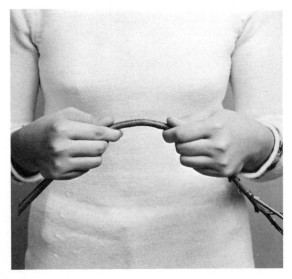

Photographs above show proper position for the hands (left), when bending stems and branches, and (right), when placing stem-ends in the *kenzan*.

Moribana

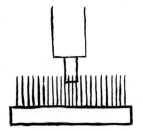

Hollow or fragile stems may be strengthened by inserting a small sturdy stick in the end.

Cut ends should be slanted.

Heika

Methods for bracing stems in tall vases.

Short lengths of stem are used for supports in *shippo*.

Examples of Various
Forms and Styles

Lichen-festooned Japanese apricot branches, fern leaves, fleshy-fingered citron, and two varieties of camellia in a Turkish blue compote.

The stately, solemn elegance of line in this arrangement is softened with a joyous note of golden color—fleshy-fingered citron—and its heaviness dispelled by the buoyancy of floating fern leaves, in this handsome arrangement made especially for celebration of the New Year.

Lichen-covered branches of Japanese apricot with camellias, and bush clover in an unglazed black container.

The black matte finish of the solidly handsome container is in tune with the dignity of the lichen-covered branches and the loveliness of camellias, two of Japan's most highly regarded traditional materials. Bush clover provides just the touch of color accent needed.

Japanese iris and marsh marigold in an amber plate.

Pale irises stand so naturally that they appear to be growing strongly upright among the graceful stems, softening leaves and dainty flowers of the marsh marigold in this portrayal of an early summer waterside.

Nandina, *small chrysanthemums, and club moss in a Kinyo (Chinese) flat basin.*

This natural scenery arrangement—traditionally Ohara—features the lavish beauty of *Nandina* in the chill of late fall. The cheerful small chrysanthemums bloom bravely through the first frost, and the club moss is used much more luxuriously than in an arrangement representing an earlier season.

Tulips and sweet-peas in a terra-cotta-ware double compote.

An expression of joyful appreciation of the arrival of spring—the bursting of March buds into fresh, colorful bloom. Massed sweet-peas slant gracefully and casually among tall tulips, to compose a harmonious blend of container and flowers.

Withered male inflorescense of Japanese sago palm, Strelitzia *and philodendron in a rectangular container with legs.*

This is a Western-style arrangement aimed at showing the color effect of the materials. Two sprays of the withered male flower clusters of the Japanese sago palm are erected slightly to the right of the center line, and two *Strelitzia* stems are placed vertically at their left. In addition, three small leaves of philodendron are used as the object and intermediary in order to enable the base to firmly hold the whole.

Poinsettias and daffodils in a wooden folk-craft bowl.

In a black shining deep bowl of rural simplicity, the crimson bracts of poinsettias and the yellow daffodil blooms glow in strong and vibrant contrast, creating an atmosphere that is both intense and primitive.

Lotus fruit and cockscomb in a glazed rectangular container.

In this arrangement, two different materials are used, the old lotus seed pods and cockscomb flowers, both of which have the feel of autumn about them. However, as a lotus is related to water, its combination with cockscomb flowers is not a realistic one. Here, several long and short lotus fruits are used and some cockscomb flowers with leaves are used in part along with them, but such a tasteful beauty is not observed in nature. Regarding the mental image projected by these two materials, it may well be said that the lotus fruits are associated with a scene from the bank of a pond in late autumn or early winter, and the cockscomb flowers with leaves remind us of a desolate winter scenery whitened with the first frost of the season.

By the use of the two materials commonly reminiscent of "autumn," I have emphasized the impression of late autumn. But most of my efforts in this work have been devoted to forming an image that, although not realistic, still conveys some traits of a real scene to one's mind.

With Fluid Movement

Japanese larch and mimosa (Acacia) *in an unglazed vase.*

In the usual color scheme arrangement there is a tendency to select brilliant floral materials and to adhere to such traditional combinations as camellia and plum. While it is both artistic and lovely, this combination has become rather ordinary, and is not in keeping with the modern mood.

In this arrangement, muted colors and an unglazed container provide a handsome new note. The abstract handling of the dead Japanese-larch branch creates a striking new line in a variation of the contrasting style. The leaves are removed from the mimosa (*Acacia*) branches, leaving the yellow flowers more dramatically revealed.

The overall effect is fresh, unusual, and satisfyingly modern and artistic.

Gingko branches, tamarisk, and calla lily in a compote.

This tall compote with a shallow bowl has an unusual shape. Even though it will not contain a large needle point holder, it is suited for heavy materials with strong lines. The gingko branches are woven around and across the bowl, and form a framework that supports the tamarisk. The calla lilies are cut short and inserted in a small holder which holds a sufficient amount of water to keep them fresh.

Gold-band lily, dried vine and green grapes in a half-moon-shaped vase with two openings.

A strong mass of vines emerges from the right opening, carefully trimmed to flow in rhythmical movement diagonally from right to left front. Two gold-band lilies help to define the movement of the vines and to provide a bright note. The solid mass and fresh green color of the grapes strengthen the focal point from which the vines flow, and are in pleasant contrast to both lilies and vines. Colors, textures and movement blend to simulate the cool atmosphere of an early summer mountainside.

Akebia and wild thistle in a rectangular footed vase.

Akebia bears attractive berries in the late autumn, but it is equally lovely in early summer, having delicate green leaves which grow in an unusually grouped formation. The vines are sturdy and curve gracefully without drooping, as well as entwining with a natural appearance; thus they may be easily arranged in a number of different styles. A careful selection of a few beautifully flowing vines is much more effective than an attempt to mass them for volume. Materials enhanced by seeds and berries are widely sought by the most discerning arrangers for unaccompanied use in artistic interpretations that are recognized and appreciated by connoisseurs.

Akebia is a mountain plant, and is at its best when combined with other materials from the same natural environment and season. Cultivated flowers such as tulips, freesias or carnations would be unsuitable. The wild thistle used here blends beautifully with both container and vines.

With Rhythm

Clematis *achenes and dahlias in a green tripod container.*

The tangled vines and *Clematis* fruits produce a gay and natural effect, to which the dahlias add vigor and color, in this freely arranged variation of the contrasting style.

Dutch rush, lily magnolia and camellias in an unglazed tall vase.

During the still-cold season of February and March, fresh green Dutch rush is a plant with much appeal for use in color scheme arrangements. Popular for styles in the non-realistic trend, Dutch rush is also ideal for a natural arrangement as used here to depict an early spring landscape in scenic design.

Behind the lily magnolia branch used as the subject of this upright style, thirteen rushes, tightly bound together at the base, form an important filler. Nine stems are similarly bound and placed in front of the subject. They are permitted to fan out slightly from their bound base, but remain erect in their natural growing position.

A single camellia forms the object, with an accompanying short leafy branch arranged low in the front of the container.

Flowering dogwood and miyako-wasure (Gymnaster saratteri) *in a green single-stem vase by Junkichi Kumakura.*

This arrangement of a single branch of flowering dogwood combined gracefully with two *miyako-wasure* blooms is an impressive reminder of the early summer season. The simplicity of design and harmonious color of the vase blend with the materials to produce the unity so essential to the success of simple arrangements.

Water Plant Arrangements

From late spring to mid-summer, the Ohara School devotes much time to the study and arrangement of waterside plant life. The observation of nature during the delicate transition of seasons leads to inspired portrayals of scenery found at the water's edge. There are fixed basic rules for the arranging of plants, and strict attention is given to the natural growth characteristics of each plant. Long-practiced traditional techniques are applied to bring about the desired perfection.

Bulrush, golden calla lily and water lily in a rectangular container.

Calla lilies are arranged compactly, as a plant, with the flowers centered among leaves extending from three sides. The tall calla serves as the subject, the leaf at the extreme right front as the secondary. The shorter flower lends variety without appearing unnatural. Three leaves are arranged behind the subject, two in front of the short flower. A whole water-lily plant, usually consisting of one flower, one rolled leaf, and one or two floating leaves, forms the object. The flower, being short-lived, must be kept very short and close to the water. Rolled leaves always appear at the outside edge of the plant. Floating leaves may be anchored in place by fixing the long, curved stems under the needlepoint holder. This helps to give the illusion of depth to the water.

Japanese yellow water-lily leaves and Iris florentina *in a shallow round basin.*

One tall iris is arranged with seven leaves to form subject and secondary, and a clump of five smaller iris leaves to form the object of this early summer natural scenery *Ikebana*. The Japanese yellow water-lily is used naturally, with two leaves in water, three above.

Both the iris and the Japanese yellow water-lily leaves are at the correct stage of maturity for the season.

Iris is a traditional Japanese plant, usually combined only with materials considered in keeping with its dignity. Therefore, since *Caladium* is a western material, this combination is new and unusual. While avoiding bright colors and heavy floral shapes, such as dahlia or gerbera, an attempt is made here to find a material both seasonally correct and complementary to the iris. The effect is cool, serene and lovely.

Bulrush and Japanese yellow water-lily in a white vase.

The technique for arranging wild-growing water plants permits more freedom of placement than that applied to cultivated material. The technique of bending stems to form interesting lines is used for non-realistic arrangements. The same technique may be applied to produce an appearance of wind-driven scenery, if some of the material—as here—is left in its erect natural state.

Three leaves and one blossom of Japanese yellow water-lily are arranged naturally, and the effect is both realistic and unusual.

Water plants require extra care for preservation. A weak solution of lead acetate may be pumped into stems, or wood ashes applied to cut ends, to help delay the yellowing of leaves. Flowers are usually more durable.

1

Japanese flowering cherry tree, Bletilla striata _(orchid), and club moss in a rectangular Kinyo (Chinese) container. Upright style._

A natural-scenery arrangement in a low bowl, having as its principal material blossoming cherry branches, is considered typically and traditionally Ohara. Even though the arrangement occupies a small container, it depicts a view of an open field, giving the impression of a cherry tree, seen from a distance, blooming above a variety of small seasonal flowers which grow in its shade.

The exacting technique of arranging a view realistically is applied to other blooming fruit tree materials as well, always with the intent to portray the tree as seen from a distance.

(1) Using the heavy flower holder (_shippo_) the subject is placed in the large opening at the rear of the holder. The secondary is slanted forward diagonally to the left, from a point as close as possible to the base of the subject, to give the appearance of having grown from a single root.

2

(2) Three fillers are added: a short, full branch between the subject and secondary, two taller ones at either side of the subject for good balance.

(3) Club moss is placed low and full in imitation of a landscape before the object is put in position, in order that the proper length of the flower in relation to the height of the cherry tree may be more easily judged.

(4) Three small clumps of _Bletilla striata_ are used to represent spring field flowers. Were they to be cut short enough to be in proper proportion to the tree, they would lose all grace and beauty; however, if clumps are short and compact, the miniature scene will not be spoiled.

3

4

Natural-Scenery Arrangement

Gold-band lily, Vaccinium ciliatum *and Chinese bellflower in a rectangular container.*
Water-reflecting style; a variation of slanting style.

Gold-band lilies are the principal material in this arrangement which calls to mind the coolness of shady mountain ravines. Realistic treatment of the lilies dictates that the stems must be left long. With the *Vaccinium ciliatum* full at the base of the lily and branching out at a low level, the effect is one of filtered sunlight in a close view of vivid mountain growth, the natural habitat, also, of the bellflower. Current trends are towards this freer, more natural handling of materials, rather than the application of strict techniques.

Careful study of the pictures is recommeneded, so that important points for natural harmony may be recognized and remembered.

Rohdea japonica, *narcissus, Japanese black pine, small chrysanthemums, and club moss in a large, rectangular basin.*

Rohdea japonica forms the subject of this natural scenery composition, in which each kind of plant is arranged according to the basic and traditional Ohara rules and techniques.

Driftwood, Japanese mountain ash and white chrysanthemums in a shallow black bowl.

A composition of Japanese mountain ash and chrysanthemums would be a simple color-scheme arrangement; however, with the addition of three pieces of driftwood arranged to provide depth, height and volume, it becomes a fresh and vigorous bit of scenery, colorful and outstanding.

Arrangements in Glass Containers

Many important features must be considered in making use of glass containers. The shape, color, texture, light-reflecting quality and transparency may all be utilized to bring out and emphasize the beauty of the materials in exactly the manner desired. Of equal importance is the handling of materials, particularly when the container is transparent. Stems and under-water portions must be cleanly and compactly arranged, as they form a visible part of the whole.

Smoke tree and Musa coccinea *in a Frenchglass container.*

Smoke tree, a tree with frothy, feathery flower clusters, grows in the South of France, and is truly French in feeling, and so is appropriate for use in a container made in the same country. The airy softness and neutral tone are in striking contrast to the strong, rather harsh lines of *Musa coccinea*.

Red and white camellias and carnations and a Monstera *leaf in two Venetian glass vases.*

Using a combination of two Venetian glass vases, large and small, carnation flowers and a *Monstera* leaf are arranged in the large one, and red and white camellias in the small one. This petite work of flower arrangement is characterized by the balanced harmony created by the joint use of a flower peculiar to Japan and a western flower that is not usually arranged with any Japanese flower.

Smilax china, *Transvaal daisy and sword fern in a green glass cup.*

For such a light and delicate container, a better harmony can be achieved by selecting light materials. By making use of the bright red nutlets and beautifully lined sprays of *Smilax china,* dark-green sword fern leaves are arranged together with short sprays of gaudy Transvaal daisies as if the fern were the leaves of the daisies. A good color effect has been attained in this work.

Lantana branches and Alocasia *leaves in a handled cut-glass vase.*

Lantana is a weedy shrub that blooms along the roadside in the southern United States. The aim of this arrangement is to offer a colorful scenic beauty, presenting a refreshingly cool feeling through leaves in a cut-glass vase with a handle.

Painted maple, clematis and withered root of Deutzia *in a French glass vase and placed on a Persian ceramic plate.*

One of the characteristics of the Japanese flower arrangement lies in setting a high value on the feeling of the seasons. This feeling is significantly deepened by associating it with a landscape.

In this work, the withered root of *Deutzia* leaning on the side of the container well reminds us of the feeling of nature on a mountain path through the greenery as if the materials were arranged with a scene of a mountain path in early summer in mind.

Small Ornamental *Ikebana*

Begonia evansiana *and great burnet in an antique copper vase.*

In this work, the black candlestand, celadon incense burner and copper vase create a sublime atmosphere and harmonize well with the flower materials.

In arranging this type of *Ikebana*, special attention should be payed to the base, so that it may not appear loose. In other words, the base must be unified to look as if the flowers have the same root. Another important operation is to place the materials in the middle of the vase. With a branch of great burnet added to the *Begonia evansiana* bearing lovely pink flowers, the sentiment of autumn is well displayed in this work.

(right)

Thistle and budded mountain ash in a roughly woven basket made by Housei.

This is a typical arrangement for a basket. When branch and grass materials are arranged together, emphasis is usually placed on the branch materials and the grass materials are used as *ashirai* (filler). In this case, however, the role of each material is just the opposite, with the lovely thistle playing the principal role.

The position is purposely reverse to represent a landscape which gives a refreshing, cool feeling in the heat of summer.

(left)

White wisteria and painted maple in a roughly woven basket made by Housei.

Baskets are often used in summer because they are especially appropriate as flower containers when seasonal mountain plants or wild plants are employed as the main materials. When a basket is to be used as a flower container, keep the following two basic rules in mind: first, use only a small number of materials and arrange them in a simple style; second, choose materials with graceful branches.

In this upright style, the beautiful white blossoms of wisteria are very attractive to the eye. Sometimes wisteria is used for a large work, but a small arrangement like this is also charming in its own way. Generally, flowers such as roses and lilies are employed as *ashirai*, but in this example painted maple is used in this way. The fresh green leaves of painted maple are arranged to balance the white blossoms of wisteria. Because of this combination, the refreshing atmosphere of early summer, the flowering season of wisteria, is well expressed.

Ground cherry, pampas grass and small chrysanthemum in a basket of Japanese folkcraft.

The red ground cherries recall childhood memories to the minds of most Japanese, for they are often found at street stalls during summer festivals.

In arranging the curiously shaped ground cherries, do not treat them seriously, but place them casually like fruit heaped in a basket. Here, pampas grass is tied up in a bundle and inserted so as to hang over the ground cherries. In contrast with the red ground cherries, small white chrysanthemums are placed in front and behind the pampas grass as if blooming in the fields.

This is an example of a slanting style of *moribana*.

Double peony and viburnum furcatum *in a brown flower container.*

The double peony, noted for its noble flowers, was considered a medicinal plant when it was introduced into Japan from China in the Nara Period (710–784).

There is little difference in appearance between double peony blooming naturally in a garden and one arranged in a vase. Its beauty remains the same wherever it may be, so technical arranging skill is unnecessary. The natural beauty of the double peony is shown to best advantage when no other materials are used in the arrangement. But dried wood or branch materials such as giant dogwood and hydrangea can be used very strikingly. In this upright style arrangement, *viburnum furcatum* brings about a graceful effect.

Materials for Better Arrangements

The selection of plants for an arrangement is often more important than the technique applied to its composition. A beautiful and impressive arrangement frequently owes its success to a fresh and sensitive combination of materials.

Pomegranate, castor-oil plant and small chrysanthemum in an old earthenware vessel from Korea.

In autumn, everything is covered with autumnal tints. Some leaves turn red, others yellow, and autumnal flowers bloom in a tender warm sunshine —but a rigorous winter is coming on.

This upright style arrangement is intended to represent autumn in China. If it gives an impression of those paintings of the Southern China school, it might fairly be called a success.

The pomegranate branch with fruit is a good material for *Ikebana*, but it requires a skilled technique. The golden red fruit of pomegranate, the large palmate bronze-green leaves and red spiny capsules of castor-oil plant and the white flowers of chrysanthemum—they all tell you something about the depth of autumn in China.

Colored maple leaves, yellow lily and small white chrysanthemums in an earthern Persian vessel.

This artless small vessel was found in an excavation in Iran. Articles from prehistoric ages seem to have special features common throughout the world. That is why the typical Japanese flowers are in harmony with this Persian vessel.

The combination of materials in this work is unique. Colored maple leaves and chrysanthemums are typical of autumn, and yellow pond lily is a summer flower, yet they are far from disharmony. This peculiar combination, harmonized with the ancient vessel, gives us an interesting impression.

Paulownia, young pine and summer chrysanthemum in a Korean vase.

This cascade style *Ikebana* is arranged in a Korean vase on which two cranes are pictured. In Japan, the light purple paulownia flowers and fresh, green pine are considered good omens. The crane, proverbially said to live a thousand years, is naturally symbolic of longevity. These materials are often combined to express good wishes at a happy event such as a nuptial ceremony.

The blooming paulownia and long leaves of pine show that it is the latter part of spring. One of the characteristics of Japanese flower arrangements is to express the change of seasons by means of flowers.

Double-flowered cherry tree and Iwaneshibori *camellia in a blue and white porcelain of the Kenryu Period in China.*

The success of this work lies in the fact that, though the cherry tree has no leaves when it blossoms, rather a disadvantage for *Ikebana* use, the camellia is loved by people for its lustrous leaves as well as its flowers. Accordingly, in this slanting style arrangement, camellia was chosen so that its green leaves would make up for the lack of leaves on the flowered cherry branches and obtain the most effective results.

Different Floral Materials in the Same Setting

One of the many enjoyable aspects of *Ikebana* is that limited selection does not impose a handicap. Restricted to the use of a single container and one principal material, it is still possible, by varying the floral accent, to achieve several different atmospheres.

Plum and lichen-festooned Japanese apricot branch in a white vase, with (A) Cattleya and (B) rape-blossoms and straw horse, an article of Japanese folkcraft.

Lichen-festooned Japanese apricot branches are often arranged with plums in order to make the plum branches look like aged trees. This is one of the traditional techniques of *Ikebana*. These two examples show that a different impression is produced by making use of different *ashirai* (fillers).

In (A), a lichen-festooned Japanese apricot branch is inserted, then budding plum trees are added as subject, secondary and intermediary stems. Finally, the *Cattleya*, well known as the best orchid, is placed as object at the mouth of the vase and the three leaves of the *Cattleya* act as intermediaries. This refined arrangement interprets no season, but it is intended to express a graceful combination of the materials.

On the other hand, in (B), the work portrays a scene in the country in the early spring. Plums and lichen-festooned Japanese apricot branches are trimmed and three rape-blossoms are added, two as intermediaries and the third as object. Lastly, the two straw horses are placed on the branches. The straw horses and yellow rape-blossoms add a touch of warmth to this simple work.

A

B

Bleached pampas grass in a three-footed container, with (A) wild aconite and cockscomb, and (B) Christmas cherry in five colors and aloe.

This unique container is ideal for grouping materials to symbolize scenery. Technique is observed only to the extent of varying the amount and kinds of materials placed in each opening. Here, wild aconite alone is placed to the left, pampas grass, aconite and cockscomb are centered, and aconite and the bleached grass are grouped in the right opening. The sunlit clouds of an October sky, mountain foliage of autumnal tints blended with green and a sharp note of bright fall floral color are vividly clear in this small picture of mountain scenery.

Christmas cherry, with its small brightly colored berries (leaves having been removed because of their perishable nature), and aloe add interesting contrast in color, form and texture to the frothy bleached pampas grass. Compared to the first example, this one has neither natural nor seasonal significance, nor does it fall into the category of non-realistic arrangement, since the materials are used in their natural form. It is a color-scheme arrangement, decorative and appealing.

Studied carefully, these examples illustrate a few of the numerous diverse themes, which virtually suggest themselves when different floral materials are introduced to the same setting.

Japanese hazelnut branch in a white, pestle-shaped vase, (A) with foxtail millet and white chrysanthemums, and (B) with amaryllis.

Japanese hazelnut is generally treated as a winter material, more attractive after its autumnal transition; however, the fresh green leaves are also appealing. To overcome the monotonous appearance of the straight slender branches with their regularly spaced leaves, they are unusually long and arranged in the slanting style. Five branches compose subject, secondary, and three fillers. Foxtail millet, symbolic of the harvest and neutral in color, stripped of its leaves, contrasts sharply with the green hazel. Two distinctive chrysanthemums strengthen the autumnal feeling.

The simplicity of Japanese hazelnut makes it particularly suitable for tea ceremony arrangements, and it is most frequently combined with materials of Japanese origin. Yet, both the foregoing seasonal arrangement and the combination of Japanese hazelnut and amaryllis, somewhat dramatic in feeling are in good taste, and suited to a Western-style room.

Golden bell with (A) red rose in a blue vase, and (B) lily magnolia in a basin decorated with red and blue Chinese patterns.

A

These two works adopt golden bells as a common material. Though the containers and styles are different, there is some resemblance in atmosphere between them.

In contrast with cherry blossoms which represent the typical Japanese concept of beauty, the quality of the golden bells is somewhat exotic. When golden bells are arranged, basic technique calls for making the most of their long, tall branches to show their colorful lines to better advantage.

In (A), the charm of the slanting arrangement of *nageire* is in the pleasing harmony achieved in the vivid contrast of yellow and red flower colors with the blue vase.

The delightful example of *moribana* in the upright style, (B), makes us feel as if we are looking at a painting of the Southern China school. An oriental atmosphere is created in both works.

B

Common unicorn plant, caladium leaves, and gladiolus in a Granadaware-vase.

An aura of excitement and vigor surrounds the Spanish container which seems to call for materials having exotic colors and distinctive lines.

Bird-of-paradise flower and carnation in a glass vase by Bianconi.

The clear strong color and shape of the bird-of-paradise flower point up the lovely original design of the Venetian container. One sharply defined line, drawn by the single leaf, dramatizes the harmonious curves of the container and of the closely arranged flowers.

Chinese scarlet eggplant and dried Hydrangea paniculata *in a Mexican container.*

A quaint piece of Taxco pottery holds Chinese scarlet eggplant ready for harvest and silvery dried hydrangeas in the simple artless manner in which they might be found growing in rural Mexico.

Autumn in Japan

Bottle gourd, cockscomb and Anthistiria arguens *(a grass) in a bamboo basket.*

Autumn is a season of gorgeous color, inspiring lavish combinations in imitation of nature's abundant and colorful harvest. To include fruit in an arrangement adds a seasonal significance that is a new approach to nature in *Ikebana*.

Sunflower seed-head and cockscomb in a tall container patterned after a Jomon design.

Modern ceramic artists recognize and imitate in today's styles the beauty of the old Jomon straw-rope patterns. *Ikebana* materials of similar texture are used with interesting results, such as this sunflower and cockscomb composition, strongly suggestive of a primitive image.

(left)
Ilex serrata *and large white chrysanthemums in a Japanese Jomon vase.*

Jomon ware (Jomondoki: earthenware with a straw-rope design) is a treasure left by Japan's first citizens, thousands of years ago, and is one of the most beautiful examples of Japanese art. To use these vessels successfully for flower arrangements requires a sensitive technique to avoid a contrived or "arty" appearance. Simplicity and elegance combined are the keynote.

Here the lovely lines of the ancient design are enhanced by a few carefully selected pieces of *Ilex serrata* and two perfect chrysanthemums, harmoniously combined.

Two kinds of plants, both suggestive of early
autumn, are selected to combine harmoniously
with this idyllically simple basket, further illus-
trating the importance of this aspect of *Ikebana*.
The vines are twisted and twined around the
basket in order to blend companionably. For a
basket of more elegant or formal design, this
rustic treatment would be inappropriate. The
basket is placed diagonally, the rear handle raised,
the front handle turned down in pleasing rhythm.
In a bamboo flower container, placed at the right
end, two large chrysanthemums are arranged as
subject and secondary, in the slanting style, to
highlight a simple bit of autumn scenery.

The addition of three kinds of materials to this
same arrangement brings about a dramatic mood
of seasonal advance. A long-stemmed lotus pod is
placed behind the subject, a short one cascades
low against the background of the basket, and a
third is seen through the mesh as it reposes inside
the basket. Two gentians and two *Patrinia* are
inserted among the other materials, with all stems
compactly together to avoid a scattered, unbalanced appearance.

Chinese-lantern plants (winter cherry), foxtail millet and small white chrysanthemums in an Akebia *vine basket.*

The abundance of the harvest season is symbolized by this voluminous arrangement in a picturesque small basket. Chinese lanterns are the principal material. One long stem is bent in a vague resemblance of a handle and a shorter stem is horizontal at the top of the basket.

Three short-stemmed foxtail-millet heads curve forward to serve as object and accompanying fillers, and the tiny chrysanthemums rise gracefully from behind the other materials.

(above)
Bleached pampas grass, hydrangea and date plum in a semi-glazed tall, handled vase.

This arrangement is an unusual example of an effective color scheme. A restrained and tranquil effect is featured in this arrangement by having its basis in the delicate nuance of white tints—the pampas grass bright and lustrous and the hydrangea subtle and shadowed. Similarly, the blue-green date plums reflect the tint of the glazed vase.

Each material possesses strong individual characteristics; yet, due to the simple style, the eye is drawn to the overall harmony of the materials and of the container.

Japanese chestnut branch, gentians and bleached summer cypress in a black vase.

This is a realistic representation of autumn mountain scenery, as both gentian and chestnut are typical of the season and habitat. The addition of the bleached cypress suggests the morning and evening mountain mists, and thus stressing the late autumn atmosphere. Composed in the upright style, the chestnut branches form subject and secondary with suitable fillers added to fill in the line. The object and companion fillers are gentians.

Grape vine and clematis in a tall glass vase.

The effect of this very decorative arrangement is a delicate and pleasing coolness. The short-lived grape leaves have been removed, and the vine arranged freely in the cascade style, to emphasize the lovely ornamental lines of the vase. With dainty white clematis as the object and the tall, balancing filler, the frosty translucent grapes tie the whole arrangement into an appealing design.

Dried Material

Dried, bleached bamboo, Japanese black pine, and roses in a modern, twice-baked free-form container.

Dried floral materials afford a superb contrast to fresh flowers and foliage, and provide much creative pleasure in endeavoring to instill such materials with life and movement.

The obvious angles are formed by bending three pieces of dried bamboo, which are placed to conform to the principal lines of the contrasting style. Short pine branches are massed to form an object; color, grace and height are provided by rose buds. The white bamboo also adds a note of purity to this clean-lined picture, strongly suggestive of the traditional Japanese congratulatory or celebrational combination of pine, bamboo and plum.

Dried China root, rhododendron and Solomon's seal (Polygonatum falcatum) *in a tall white vase.*

In the foregoing arrangement the root material was used ornamentally. Here, a natural atmospheric effect is achieved with China root. The feeling is one of craggy, winter-bare mountains, of melting snows, first spring sprouts and early blooms.

Ordinarily in using root-materials for *nageire* arrangements, a realistic manner is observed; however, occasionally an abstract treatment more strongly suggests the desired environment and atmosphere.

(above)

Dried-root-material, Asparagus myriocladus, *and* Dendrobium *in a tall compote.*

Here is an effective blending of material and container, the volume and shape of the deformed root being displayed to advantage, suspended against the tall, bare column of the compote, as the focal point of this arrangement.

In the shallow, half-moon-shaped basin of the compote, two sprays of *Dendrobium* form the subject and secondary of the contrasting style, with fillers of *Asparagus myriocladus* softly concealing the point where stems and the root formation emerge from the container.

The leaves and dried flowers of artichoke with Iceland poppy in a U-shaped vase of original design by Sango Uno.

Two center openings form part of the unusual design of this vase, which also has two small openings at the top.

To achieve a successful arrangement in this container, materials and vase must be merged into a single harmonious design. Five artichoke flowers fall forward gracefully from the top center opening. Silvery artichoke leaves emerge from the top left opening of the vase, to blend with the soft shades of the container and the dried flowers for a subdued color-effect. Bright, butterfly-yellow poppies provide an important accent.

Actually, the materials have been handled simply and naturally, rather than artistically. The distinctive container and the unusual texture, color and form of the materials provide the artistry in this unique original design.

Non-realistic Arrangements

Ikebana artists, by disregarding the natural characteristics of plants, and endeavoring to bring out and develop the unusual beauty found in ordinary colors and common materials, are exploring a new and exciting field of *Ikebana*.

Mitsumata, *gladiolus and asparagus a white porcelain vase.*

This non-realistic flower arrangement aims at the decorative beauty that may be brought about by contrast in feeling between the color and the shape of the material. This is the point of interest in a work of art created through the use of a particular contrast, such as that between the elegantly simple and the strikingly vivid, the strong and the weak, and that between markedly contrasting colors.

The photograph shows a vertical style arrangement composed by decoratively arranging the red of the fresh and vivid gladiolus flowers and the green of the asparagus leaves, that are added to the base material, *mitsumata* (*Edgeworthia chrysantha*), which is of a fine white color and is light and plain in feeling.

Winged spindle-tree branches and five daffodils in a three-legged vase.

The branches of the winged spindle-tree (*Euonymus alata*) are suggestive of rusty iron wire. Having little plant-like aspect in its appearance, this is one of the most suitable materials for non-realistic flower arrangements.

In general, there are two methods for inventing the devices to make a plant assume the appearance of some other material in a non-realistic flower arrangement: one is to find a material already with suitable characteristics and the other is to change the characteristics when processing the materials. Both techniques are inseparably related to each other, and either method may assert itself according to the features of the work of art. If you can find a material already satisfactory at the time of selection, you will accomplish your flower arrangement quickly and this will facilitate good results.

This work aims at indicating an artificial and dynamic movement different from the natural movement of branches of a tree. The branches of winged spindle-tree suggestive of rusty iron wire are bent to the left and right and are arranged to indicate complicated movement brought about by the violent mixture of different branches.

With Pieces of Wood

Old mossy or lichen-covered trunks and branches are good materials for use in composing forms and frameworks for arrangements. They may be utilized as semipermanent containers, with periodic changes of floral material. Large branches for exhibition pieces and small bits for charming table arrangements are equally appropriate backgrounds for fresh flowers, with each change creating a new aspect of beauty.

(right)
With small circular straw mats, pine and camellia.

(below)
With foxtail millet and camellias.

With Vines

Small and passive arrangements, or large ones lacking in movement, may be enhanced by the use of vines. The result can be a new, softer line, a rhythmical life and seeming increase in size.

When vines are used as materials, it is important to choose long ones, placing emphasis on line and movement. In this upright style *Ikebana*, the three long branches of bittersweet accentuate the whole arrangement. The longest one extends upward gracefully and the others curve downward and swing to the right. The highlight of this work is the striking color contrast between the crimson mass of cockscomb and the large-flowered white chrysanthemums in which far advanced autumn is well expressed.

Cockscomb, chrysanthemum and bittersweet in a celadon porcelain basin.

(right)
Joseph's coat, Eulalia-grass and bittersweet in a bamboo basket.

The Joseph's coat, which is of the same family as cockscomb, and the bittersweet depict deepening autumn. The atmosphere between the work on the left side and this one appears the same, but the Joseph's coat has basically different characteristics from the cockscomb. First of all, it has no flowers and is comprised of leaves alone. Next, it spreads around, while the cockscomb constitutes a voluminous mass. Furthermore, the Joseph's coat is sometimes arranged in a slanting style, but the cockscomb should always be arranged upright.

Paying careful attention to the lines of the vines, and making the most of them, can assure interesting effect.

In this upright style arrangement, the natural curve of the branches of bittersweet plays an important role, giving a vigorous impression.

THE SOGETSU SCHOOL

By Sofu Teshigahara

Translated by Hisako Komine

Of several popular modern schools of *Ikebana*, the Sogetsu School was established in 1925 by Sofu Teshigahara, the author of this chapter. Like the Ohara School, the Sogetsu School created its own new styles in breaking away from the classic Ikenobo style, and in so doing, it experienced the same objections and hindrances from the more conservative elements. Today, the Sogetsu School emphasizes freedom of expression in flower arrangement while still conforming to some of the criteria of traditional *Ikebana*. However, it is the aim of this relatively new school to continue its education of the public of the fact that *Ikebana*, like other arts, must create new styles in order to progress. *Ikebana* must not confine itself to old form and styles but must strive to develop new and original expressions of style.

The Sogetsu School, like all creative arts, has developed many new forms, but all are based on the concept that *Ikebana* is an art form most closely related to sculpture. As can be seen from the photographs that accompany this chapter, some forms express the natural state of flowers whereas others stress humanistic, subjective feelings. In other words, in some compositions the arranger may place the main emphasis on the flower, with his own subjective feelings subdued. In other compositions, the subjectivity of the arranger is prominently expressed, sometimes to such an extent that the natural element becomes of minor importance. In the selection of themes, then, the arranger has his choice of wholly objective or wholly subjective forms. Some of the innovations of the Sogetsu School, in its departures from traditional style, are the creation of arrangements without containers, the use of withered plants and materials, the development of free-style forms, the use of artificial materials, and, in general, the development of the concept of the unity of flower arrangement with sculpture—*Ikebana* of this school may be defined as sculpture with flowers.

In spite of his many departures from and innovations upon more traditional styles, Sofu Teshigahara, Headmaster of the Sogetsu School, emphasizes with great earnestness that the forms and styles of the Sogetsu School are truly the expressions of *Ikebana*, with all the depth of symbolism and of philosophical meaning inherent in that term. To be more specific, the style of the Sogetsu School is true *Ikebana*, an art form most closely allied with sculpture, and is not simply flower decoration in the Western sense.

W.C.S.

Ikebana in the Sogetsu School

SIZE OF ARRANGEMENTS

The standard size is about three feet high. Some are small enough to be carried in one hand while others are so large that several people are required to carry it. Some measure 10–15 feet high.

COMBINATION OF FLOWERS

It is the principle of the Sogetsu School to combine two kinds of flowers; however, there are instances in which one kind only is used. At other times, three kinds of flowers are used.

However, it can be said that the most effective arrangement can be obtained by using one kind of tree and one kind of grass. Frequently, the use of several kinds gives the impression of disorder.

WHEN NO CONTAINER IS NEEDED

There are cases in which no container is used. The fundamental rule of *Ikebana* is to "use a certain vase for a certain flower." It must be noted, however, that the Sogetsu School does not use containers in some cases. This style has become very popular lately but it is a relatively new trend. It was first introduced by the Sogetsu School about 30 years ago. It is a style that makes possible the free expression of creative flower arrangement. It is expected that this style will become more popular in the future.

THE USE OF WITHERED PLANTS

Fundamentally, fresh natural plants are used as the principal material; however, the Sogetsu School uses withered grass, dead trees and roots. In the beginning, objections were made to the use of withered grass, roots and dead trees; however, it came to be gradually recognized that beauty does not exist in fresh plants only. Today, withered grass and boughs can be purchased at flower shops in the U.S. and Europe.

BEAUTY OF LINE

The Sogetsu School of flower arrangement is noted for the beauty of its lines.

It is not easy to explain the beauty of flower arrangement. However, one of the outstanding features of the Sogetsu School is the beauty of line.

The materials must be so arranged that the lines of the branches, stems, leaves and trunks will be beautiful from any angle. This can be clearly understood by observing the examples shown herein.

In flower arrangement, technique is not the only important thing. However, techniques are indispensable to artistic flower arrangement. Therefore, it is essential to master the essential techniques in order to be able to fully express the beauty of line.

Students are requested to study the examples by keeping these points in mind.

Examples of Sogetsu *Ikebana*

Time of Balmy Breeze

Japanese iris and fullmoon maple in a flat basket. Theme of natural atmosphere in Ikebana.

Dawn

(right)

Japanese quince and white chrysanthemums in Satsuma *pottery. The arrangement creates bright pleasure from the harmony of red and white.*

Joy

(below)

White Japanese apricot and red camellias in a low blue basin gives a near-the-pond atmosphere.

Brothers

(right)
A composition of sun-flower and Eucalyptus in white porcelain. Flower arrangements may often express human figures.

Dance of Flowers

Oriental bittersweet and Anthurium *in a shiny black vase creates graceful movements of crossing lines and color combination of beautiful flowers.*

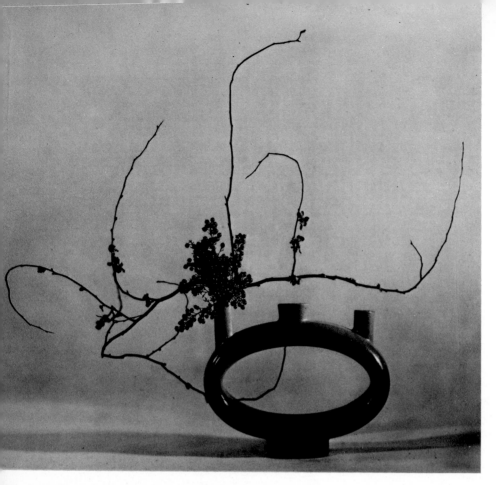

Melody of a Flute

Japanese quince and Nandina *berries in celadon porcelain.*
This arrangement expresses clear delicate rhythm.

Environment of *Ikebana*

Here are several works harmonizing with one another. Porcelain plate—handwriting of Sogu in frame. Strelitzia, cypripedium orchid and winter jasmine in bamboo container. Maple branch and Anthurium in Picasso pot. Two sculptures by Sofu.

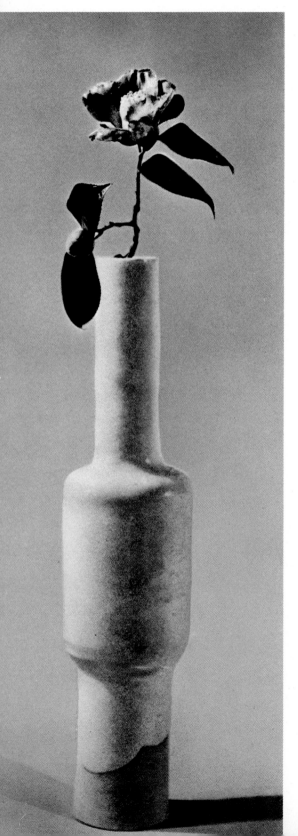

Steady Gaze

(left)
A single red camellia in a tall white porcelain vase. The single branch expresses sublimity. The first and second main stems are not used; only the third main stem is used.

Blessing

(right)
A composition of Japanese white birch, pine, camellia and berries of "Sankirai" *(Similax china).*

Message from the Hills

(above)

A montage of rural fields is portrayed by driftwood, leaves of Cymbidium orchid, and berries of Smilax china.

Imagination

(left)

The softness of fur flowers and feminine gracefulness is suggested by dried spikes of Eularia grass arranged with Anthurium in a golden basin.

Delight

(right)

Red Japanese quince in a glass vase. This form expresses delicate movement.

Winter Sunshine

A composition of Polyanthus narcissus *and white camellia.*
These unsophisticated flowers express tranquility.

Perplexity

Hydrangea and tulips in a red glass basin.
A representative form suitable for any
room.

Movement of Water

Sallow (goat willow) in an iron basin. The Sogetsu School of Ikebana *places emphasis on the expressing of beauty of line.*

Duet

Sallow (goat willow) and hydrangea in a square china basin.

Spring

(left)
Reeve's Spiraea in a white and blue basin.

Children

(below)
Tulips in a green basin. Any type of flowers provide graceful lines and can be appreciated from any view.

Birth

Chinese cabbage, lemons and berries of Smilax china. *Vegetables and fruits may also be used for* Ikebana.

Sweet Breeze

Aspidistra leaves and chrysanthemums. The surface of
water expresses the essence of Ikebana.

Vigor

Driftwood and white camellias in a cinnabar unglazed vase.
According to the material selected, an unlimited strength
may be expressed.

Garden

In this composition of Japanese **Mahonia** *and red roses in a light blue and brown basin the identity of the three main stems are clearly visible.*

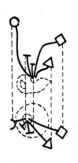

Fundamental Forms of the Sogetsu School

Form 1

    Moribana...shallow bowl and needle-point holder are used. Refer to examples No. 1 and No. 2.

Form 2

    Nageire...Perpendicular or upright vase. Holders not used. Refer to examples No. 3 and No. 4.

Flower arrangement lessons start with *moribana* and advance to *nageire*.

It must be noted here that there are other special forms in the Sogetsu School. For example, there are forms that use no container. Also, there is a combination of *moribana* and *nageire*. These are all variations of the two fundamental forms. The important thing, therefore, is to master the fundamental forms so that variations can be created.

Before starting practice in flower arrangement, it is essential to have a full grasp of the fundamentals. This applies to both the *moribana* and *nageire*.

Needle-point Holder (*Kenzan*)

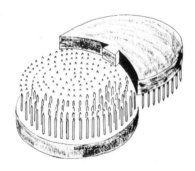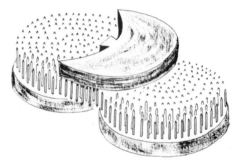

Use of Needle-point Holder

For twigs.

For flowers and grass.

Principal and Subordinate Stems

All Sogetsu School flower arrangements are composed of the principal stem and subordinate stems. The principal stem is the center of the arrangement. The subordinate stems are complements.

Three Main Stems

There are three main stems and each has a name. They are:

Shin...the principal and most important stem; it is the longest of the three main stems.

Soe...the second stem of medium length.

Hikae...the third stem and the shortest of the three stems.

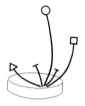

First Main stem (Shin)

Second Main stem (Soe)

Third Main stem (Hikae)

Length of Main Stems

The most important thing is to decide the length of the *shin* stem. The length appropriate for the vase must be decided. The length of the *soe* is determined from the length of the *shin* stem. Likewise, the length of the *hikae* stem is determined from the length of the *soe* stem.

How to Measure Vase

Add depth of vase to diameter of vase.

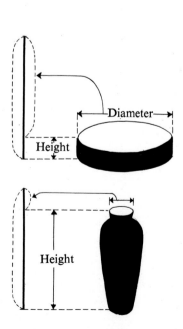

Height — Diameter

Height

229

Illustrations of Main Stems
and Subordinate Stems

In Sogetsu School, the following illustrations
are used to explain flower arrangement.

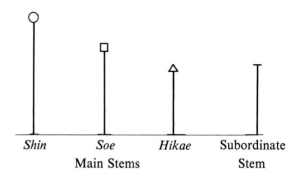

Shin   *Soe*   *Hikae*   Subordinate

Main Stems   Stem

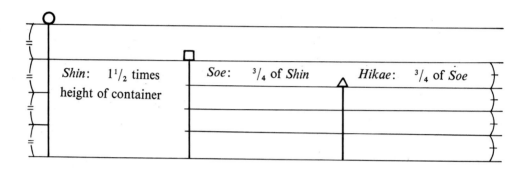

Shin: $1^1/_2$ times height of container

Soe: $^3/_4$ of *Shin*

Hikae: $^3/_4$ of *Soe*

Length of *Shin*

The standard length of the *shin* stem is 1.5 times the measurement of the vase. However, when it is a large flower arrangement, make length of *shin* two times the vase measurement. For a small arrangement, make *shin* the same length as measurement of vase.

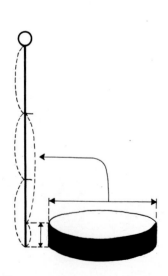

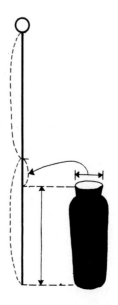

The length of the subordinate stems should always be shorter than the main stem.

The following illustration shows the main stems and subordinate stems in *moribana* arrangement.

Main stems and subordinate stems in *nageire* arrangement.

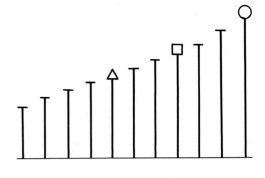

Moribana

Nageire

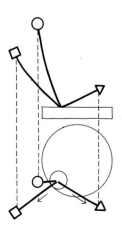

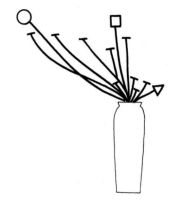

Direction and Angle of Principal Stem

Generally, the principal stem slants forward from diagonally left or right.

Examples of direction and angle of principal stem in *moribana*:

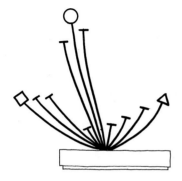

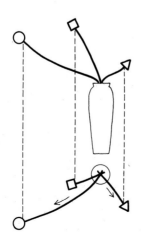

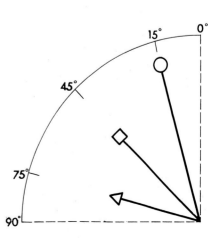

The right illustration shows the angle of the main stem to the other stems.

Preservation of Cut Flowers

Cutting Stems in Water

The Sogetsu School places great emphasis on the correct handling of cut flowers. This is the method of cutting the stems while holding them in water.

Flower taken from trees and from plants in the garden should be cut again in water.

Flower purchased from the florist should also be cut in water.

When arranging flowers, each stem should be cut in water.

The life of plants can be increased by cutting in water. Cut the stem at an angle while holding it under water. Do not cut the stem by holding the flower in the air because air will enter the stem and the flower will lose the strength to absorb water. Withered plants can be revived by cutting the stems in water.

Charring Treatment

There is the method of charring the end of the stem. It is important to cut the stem in water before giving this treatment.

Boiling Water Treatment

First wrap the flowers with paper to protect the blooms and then boil the stems in hot water for a few minutes.

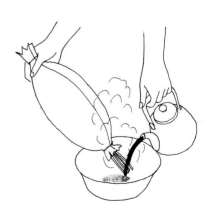

Chemical Treatment

Alcohol, acetic acid, peppermint oil or tincture of cayenne may be applied to the cut ends. Do not forget to cut the ends before giving this treatment.

Flower arrangements should not be placed in a very warm place or where the wind is strong. It is better to forget to give additional water than to put the arrangement in a windy place.

The best time to cut garden flowers is during the early morning. Place the flowers in a bucket of water immediately after cutting.

Method of Practice—*Moribana*

There is a special arrangement form for practicing. This is called the fundamental Upright Style arrangement. Since this is the fundamental form, the student is advised to practice this form over and over again in order to master the basic design.

This form can be practiced by using any kind of flower. It is not necessary to use the same flower as that used in the example.

The important thing is to determine the right length of the stems according to the vase. Care should also be used in determining the length of the subordinate stems.

How to Secure Stems

The most important thing to do in *moribana* is to secure the stems on the needle-point holder.

As shown in the illustration, all stems must be securely held by the needle-point holder.

How to Use the *Kenzan*

Cut end of stem at angle and press into needle-point holder. Press stem straight into holder, then slant to desired angle. Cut flower stems straight.

When the branch is too heavy for the *kenzan*, use another one for weight as shown in illustration.

The student must practice until he is able to place stems in the holder without any trouble. The reason why *Ikebana* is difficult for some people is because they are not skilled in securing the stems in the needle-point holder. Skill is acquired by continuous practice. Since the matter of placing the stems securely in the needle-point holder is one of the fundamentals of flower arrangement, the student must practice until he becomes skilled.

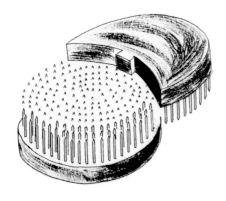

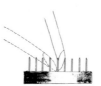

For twigs.

For flowers and grass.

Correct Positions

In the Sogetsu School of flower arrangement, there are four positions to place the needle-point holders and one of these positions is selected.

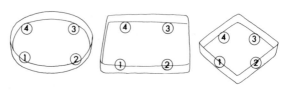

EXAMPLE 1

Fundamental Upright Style

Materials: *Branches of oak*
Chrysanthemums
Vessel: *White porcelain vase*
(shallow bowl)

Ikebana form: Fundamental upright style

First (*shin*) stem: ⎫
Third (*soe*) stem: ⎬ oak branches

Second (*hikae*) stem: chrysanthemum
Position: 1

Care of Flowers

Illustration 1 shows flowers which were not treated and Illustration 2 shows flowers properly treated.

Inspect flowers carefully before arranging. Cut off all dead and discolored leaves and faded blossoms. That is, remove all parts that are not perfect. A comparison of the examples aptly shows the importance of proper treatment of the materials. The picture also shows the technique of cutting one branch into a number of branches. Flower arrangement using flowers that have not been treated properly will appear lifeless and ineffective.

Illustration 3 shows the *shin* stem in place. Illustrations 4 and 5 show the second and third stems in their places. These three main stems

Remove all superfluous parts and place emphasis on one point.

compose the outline of the arrangement. Illustration 6 is the completed arrangement. It is important for the student to study the way in which the three main stems are arranged. Study the general effect and balance between the oak branches and flowers.

Compare the front view with the plane view to study the way the stems are placed.

The student must become thoroughly familiar with the fundamental upright style since this is the base for all other forms. The important thing is to acquire a thorough understanding of the fundamental form; the superficial appearance of the flower is of secondary importance.

The kind of material to be used is not so important; just think of it as a tree, a branch or a blade of grass.

1. *Untreated flowers.*

2. *Treated flowers.*

3. *First main stem in place.*

4. *Second main stem in place.*

5. *The three main stems in place.*

6. *Subordinate stems added.*

Loquat branches in bloom are arranged in a white china basin. As can be seen, only one branch is used in some frame of fundamental upright style.

This example of the fundamental upright style is composed of branches of Japanese quince and camellias in a black basin.

EXAMPLE 2

Fundamental Inclined First Stem Form

Materials: *Japanese cypress*
Chrysanthemums
Vessel: *Blue celadon porcelain tray (low)*
Ikebana form: Fundamental inclined first stem
form

First (*shin*) stem: }
Second (*soe*) stem: } Japanese cypress

Third (*hikae*) stem: chrysanthemums
Position: 3

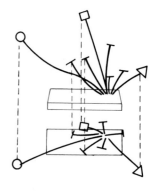

Illustration 1...main stem only.
Illustration 2...second stem put into place.
Illustration 3...third stem in place.

The fundamental inclined first-main-stem style is the base for all inclined main-stem forms just as the fundamental upright style is the base for all upright forms.

The basic forms of the Sogetsu School are the upright style and inclined style. All other forms are variations of these two basic forms. In the fundamental inciined main stem form, the positions of the first stem and second stem have been interchanged with the positions of the first and second stems of the fundamental upright form; there is no change in the treatment of the third (*hikae*) stem.

Students thoroughly familiar with the fundamental upright form will have no trouble in understanding the significance and method of interchanging the main and second stems. It will be interesting to note the remarkable changes brought about by alternating these stems.

It is for these reasons that the thorough understanding of the fundamental upright form is essential. The fundamental inclined main stem form is obtained by partial changes in the fundamental upright form.

In the fundamental upright form, the main stem is placed in an upright position and the second stem is inclined. In the inclined form, the main stem is placed at an inclined angle and the second stem is placed upright.

In both forms, the third stem is placed in the same way.

4

7

5

8

6

Illustrations 4, 5, 6 … subordinate stems added.
Illustrations 7 and 8… subordinate stems added to third stem.
Illustration 8…   completed flower arrangement.

Method of Practice—*Nageire*

Moribana is arranged in a low bowl using a needle-point holder while *nageire* uses an upright vase with narrow mouth; therefore, no holder is required. There is no change in the use of the three main stems and method measuring the length of the stems; however, there is naturally a difference in the way the stems are secured.

In order to master the Sogetsu School of flower arrangement, the student must become thoroughly familiar with both *moribana* and *nageire*.

The proper order of practice is to start with *moribana* and to advance to *nageire*. It must be remembered that the techniques of *nageire* are more difficult and complex than those used in *moribana*. Skill is acquired only through untiring application and practice.

Securing Stems in Place

The root of the main stem must reach to the bottom of the container (vase). Split the end of the main stem and insert a piece of branch to serve as holder. For the best results, use a sturdy piece of branch to hold the stem in place.

Place the second stem securely in place in the same way. Illustrations 1 and 2 show the form of the stems as they appear in place and the way the stems look inside the vase. Placing stems in the vase in this way appears easy; however, it is important to practice this technique until one is skilled.

EXAMPLE 3

Materials: *Branches of Japanese quince*
            Red roses
Vessel: *White celadon porcelain vase*
Form: *Inclined style*
Main stem: } branches of Japanese quince
Second stem: }
Third stem: red roses

5

4

Illustration 1... Main stem secured in place with piece of stick as holder.

Illustration 2... Second stem placed in position.

Illustration 3... Third stem is added and the framework of the arrangement is completed.

Illustration 4... Subordinate stem for the third main stem is added.

Illustration 5... Another subordinate stem is added to the third main stem.

EXAMPLE 4

Materials: *Branches of azalea*
Roses
Vessel: *Bizen vase*
Form: *Inclined style*
First and second stems: azalea branches
Third stem: roses

Illustration 1... *Main stem in place.*
Illustration 2... *First and second stems secured in place.*
Illustration 3... *Subordinate branches added to third stem. Arrangement is completed.*

3

EXAMPLE 5

Materials: *Camellias*
Vessel: *White porcelain vase*
Form: *Inclined style*

First second and third stems: Camellia branches. This example shows the method of separating one branch into several branches to form one complete arrangement.

Illustration 2 shows the original camellia branch cut into three separate branches to form one arrangement.

3

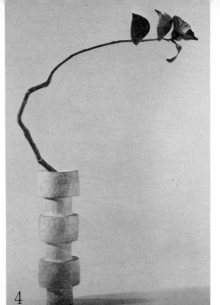

4

5

Original Arrangements—Free Style

In practicing the fundamental forms, it is best to follow the lines of the examples closely. The points to be kept in mind are:

1. Treatment of materials
2. Measurement of materials
3. Securing stems in place
4. Direction of stems
5. Angles of incline
6. Addition of subordinate stems

These points must be kept in mind in both the *moribana* and *nageire* styles. Efforts should be made to quickly discern the changes in the flowers.

Students of the Sogetsu School should not be satisfied with merely copying the example forms. Efforts should be made toward individuality.

There are many variations; however, they are obtained by changing the treatment of the position, direction, angle or length of the three main stems.

First, the fundamental forms must be mastered. Then, some time must be given to the practice of making variations in the three main stems. The basic forms may be used as a guide to creating original forms. It is not necessary to use the same vase and materials in practice for creative style.

Clear Mind

Chrysanthemums in a brilliant blue basin.

Morning

(right)
Japanese quince and Bouvardia *in a blue striped vase.*

After the Rain

(below)
Fullmoon maple and peonies in a white china vase.

Illusion

Torch lily and hydrangeas in a low basin.

Purple and Cinnabar

A composition of asparagus fern and Clematis in a white and vermillion glass vase.

Symphony

Smilax china, *celosia and* Caladium *in a slim yellow and white glass vase.*

Bright Eyes

Sunflowers and a black vine in a white vase with two mouths.

252

From Applied Form to Free Style

The "Four-front" Style

This style of flower arrangement is used when the arrangement is to be viewed from all directions.

Naturally, there must be no front side or back side to the composition.

The branches must be arranged carefully so that no branch hinders the view of the other sections of the arrangement.

Fountain

Snapdragon, daffodills and Asparagus cochinensis *in a light blue basin*.

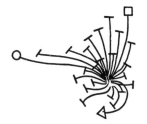

Ripples

An arrangement of Japanese iris and Bulrush in a white china basin.

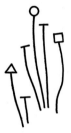

Mid-Day Dream

Water lilies in a white china basin.

Group of Maidens

An arrangement of Asparagus cochinensis
and sweet peas in a glass basin.

Dewy Mountain Lane

(below)
Goldband lily and false spirea arranged in a white vase and basin around a piece of driftwood.

Spring in Ancient Capital

(right)
Branches of Japanese witch hazel and red camellias in a Celudo porcelain vase.

Animation

*Japanese quince and mimosa in a golden
and clear glass vase.*

Sun Rise

*Weeping willow and sweet peas arranged
in dark-brown, two-mouthed vase.*

Maternal Love

(left)
Anthurium and Smilax in a
hanging vase.

Evening Moon

(right)
White Japanese quince and
red camellias in a bamboo wall
vase.

Friendship

Eucalyptus and Dutch iris in a light blue
glass basin, as seen from above.

Gratitude

(below)
Clematis arranged on a coral lacquered tray.

Harmony

(at bottom of page)
Asparagus myriocladus and sweet peas arranged on a bright blue tray.

Christmas

A holiday arrangement of holly, poin-settia and gold lace in an iron ship.

Christmas

(above)
White chrysanthemums, Chinese horse brier (Smilax china), gold lace and glass balls in a white china vase.

Christmas

(right)
Holly and colored glass balls brighten a four-legged black basin.

Ikebana for Decorative Purposes

If stunningly different style of *Ikebana* is desired for special occasions like Christmas, gold and silver braid, glass balls and other gay decorations can be selected to create the Christmas atmosphere. Candles can also be used.

Artificial flowers, gold and silver braid, painted plants, candles and colored bulbs, gold and silver trays, sand, pebbles, feathers, stems, branches, garlands of flowers and wreaths can all be used effectively.

Christmas

Carnations and artificial poinsettia in a china vase.

Christmas

A gold star surrounded by holly in a tall, red glass vase.

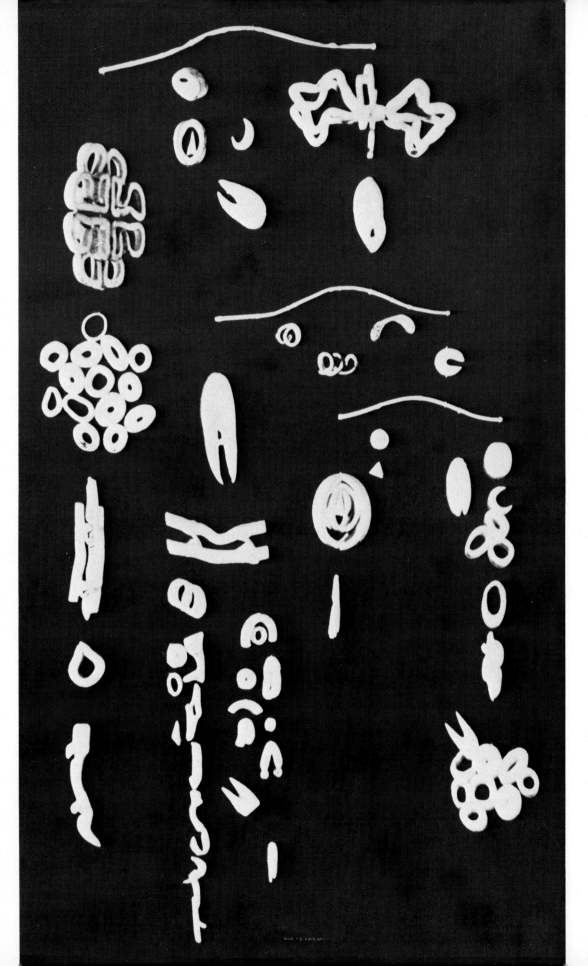

Mobile and Relief Style Arrangements

In the mobile style of flower arrangement, there is a sense of movement in the arrangement. This effect is obtained by hanging branches, fruits, withered grass and leaves. Also, driftwood can be used with great effect.

Flower arrangement in relief effect can be regarded as wall *Ikebana* or picture *Ikebana*. Use Cellophane tape to arrange flowers in a frame.

Happy Family

Bamboo mobile.

Face

Wheat spikes.

Home

Relief of pine-cones and dried leaves.

Making Flower Vases

With only a little trouble, anyone can make his own flower vase. Use initiative to fashion a vase out of a piece of bamboo by cutting an opening to the desired size.

A vase can be made by carving a piece of stone.

A sheet of iron can be shaped into an interesting vase.

Empty tins, bottles, boxes and sea shells can also be used in interesting ways.

(right)
Anthurium and
Monstera *in an*
iron vase.

Super-size Flower Arrangement

The size of the room as well as its color must be considered when arranging flowers, as the arrangement must be in complete harmony with its surroundings.

Flower arrangements for a large hallway must have force and vigor. Special consideration must be given to the selection of the container; again its color and shape must harmonize with the surroundings.

Large Japanese Room

Entrance of Large Building

An arrangement of driftwood and camellias.

A large work of pine, Citrus junos *and Japanese cedar.*

Artificial Beauty

The beauty of a flower arrangement owes much to the skill and technique of the arranger. The conception and skill behind the work are points that must be noted.

As has been pointed out repeatedly, skill is acquired only by practice and effort. This is a central point emphasized by the Sogetsu School.

(right)
Bleached broom cypress and red leaves in a black vase.

(left)
Bleached broom cypress, receptacles of Indian lotus, and Chinese horse brier berries in a violet colored vase.

(right)
Aspidistra leaves arranged in a black basin.

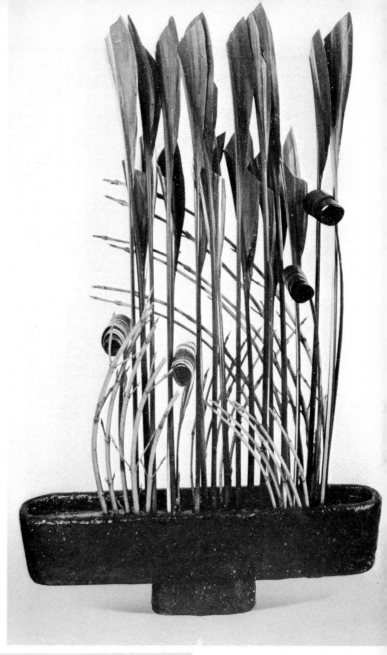

(below)
Winged spindle tree branches and camellias in a black and brown vase.

277

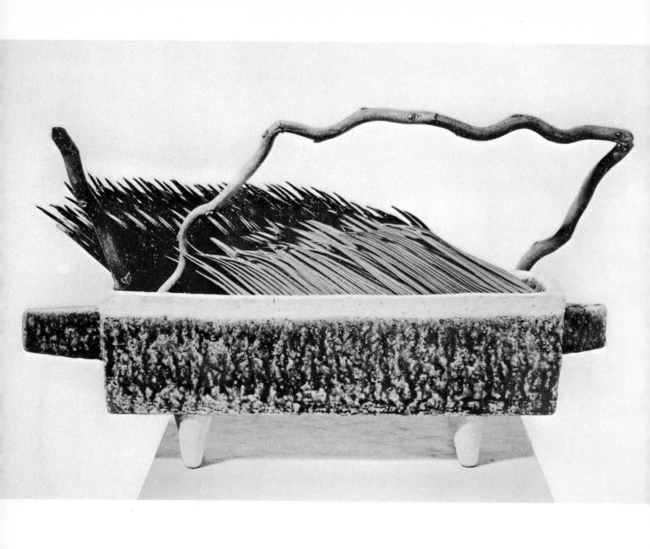

(above)
*A white mulberry branch and Cycas leaves
arranged in an Iga pottery vase.*

Miniature *Ikebana*

A miniature *Ikebana* style also exists in the Sogetsu School. The size of flower arrangements can range from extra large to these miniatures.

Miniature *Ikebana* emphasizes the use of a single flower petal, a pebble or a blade of grass, things that are often overlooked.

Various Miniature *Ikebana*

(below)
Japanese maple and wild scarlet lily in an
eared bowl made in the Edo Period.

(above)
Bleached weeping willow, Japanese
beautyberry and a rose arranged in a sake
bottle.

Camellia and Irex serrata *in a bamboo tube.*

Ikebana as Sculpture

Ikebana is sculpture with flowers and plants. It has a three-dimensional effect and must not be regarded as separated from sculpture, as such an idea might delay the progress of the flower-arrangement art. In the Sogetsu School, it is essential to regard flower arrangement and sculpture as one. The Sogetsu School is expanding its studies into many fields so that the student is not confined within just the narrow confines of flower arrangement. A new form of sculpture is being developed by the Sogetsu School—a new style called Sculpture *Ikebana*. We believe that great developments will eventually be seen in this direction.

Statice and Transvaal daisy in an ironwork.

Artichoke and Asparagus myriocladus *with a dog-shaped ironwork.*

Windows of Mythology

A wooden sculpture covered with copperplates and leadplates.